AF248636

Werner Weidenfeld

America and Europe:
Is the Break Inevitable?

Werner Weidenfeld

America and Europe:
Is the Break Inevitable?

Bertelsmann Foundation Publishers
Gütersloh 1996

Die Deutsche Bibliothek – CIP-Einheitsaufnahme

Weidenfeld, Werner:
America and Europe : Is the Break Inevitable? /
Werner Weidenfeld. – Gütersloh :
Bertelsmann Foundation, 1996
ISBN 3-89204-249-7

© 1996 Bertelsmann Foundation Publishers, Gütersloh
Responsible: Dirk Rumberg
Editors: Annette Heuser, Andreas Klaßen, Gabriele Schroers
Translation: Bonnscript, Textredaktions- und Übersetzungs-
dienste GmbH, Bonn
Copy editor: Brigitte Neuparth
Production editor: Beate Plümer
Cover design: HTG Werbeagentur, Bielefeld
Cover photo: Tony Stone Bilderwelten,
Mauritius Die Bildagentur, Bavaria Bildagentur,
Imagine Fotoagentur, Zefa, IFA-Bilderteam
Typesetting: Utesch Satztechnik GmbH, Hamburg
Print: Fuldaer Verlagsanstalt GmbH
ISBN 3–89204–249–7

Table of contents

Cultural split with America or the beginning of a new transatlantic success Story?

It would be naive to expect German-American friendship and the Euro-American partnership to have been unaffected by the ending of the East-West conflict. No doubt the relationship will continue to be viewed through rose-colored glasses for a while yet, but one only needs to look below the surface to realize that the transatlantic relationship has been subjected to considerable erosion. A variety of factors – declining interest and the loss of personal links as a new generation takes over, a tendency for politicians to turn inwards and focus on domestic affairs, hazier definitions of geographical entities, surprising changes in political standpoints – all mean that the relationship between Germany, Europe and America is no longer based on certainties of the kind that have existed for fifty years. Links across the Atlantic have almost inevitably been sucked into the radical upheavals occurring in world politics since the end of the Cold War, yet, at the same time, those same links must provide new answers to new challenges.

In terms of communication theory, what is happening is a disintegration of the stabilizers and filters required for information-processing – the dominance of world politics by large blocks and their confrontational relations has gone and with it the antagonisms, stereotypes and political rhetoric that used to provide collective orientation for the "West."

In future, therefore, a positive rationale for the partnership between Europe and America will have to be found. It is no longer possible merely to rely on a clear demarcation from one's potential opponents within a static global conflict. For some time, attitudes within the transatlantic relationship will continue to be shaped by the unique success story shared over the last fifty years. But the old loyalties will no longer be enough to provide the necessary political and analytical parameters for the next phase in Euro-American cooperation. Sooner or later, Germany, Europe and America will find themselves redefining their interests.

It would be desirable if this were a process that resulted in positive gains for both sides. But it is perfectly possible that the opposite will happen – in terms of foreign policy, a drifting apart of the partners under the influence of the centrifugal forces of international crisis; in terms of economic policy, an escalation of transatlantic trade rivalries; and in social terms, the gradual disappearance of the two partners over the transatlantic horizon.

This negative scenario would mean more than just a difficult restructuring of foreign policy priorities for Europe and the USA. In fact, it would shake the very foundations of the European and the American self-image. Historically speaking, each partner has always formed part and parcel of the other's identity. The commitment of the Americans to the reconstruction of Europe after the Second World War is, particularly for the Germans, a central element in our collective consciousness. And the contribution made by Germans and Europeans in general to the development of the USA is a leitmotif running through the American psyche which transcends all demographic and ethnic change.

Thus, for both sides, the loss of their transatlantic partner would do more than just inflict damage in foreign policy terms – it would lead to a cultural split with disastrous consequences. So if the redefinition of the transatlantic relationship is to succeed it has to offer both partners not only a common agenda in practical terms, but also a redefinition of their own identity which incorporates the partner on the other side of the Atlantic.

For there to be a new era of transatlantic cooperation, the political elite of Europe and America will have to display the sort of vision shown by the founding fathers of the post-war order. A reorientation of the relationship is inevitable, but it remains to be seen whether it will be possible to develop further this valuable transatlantic friendship and enable it to operate effectively under new conditions. It is against this backdrop that this publication analyzes the background of the transatlantic relationship and considers the prospects for reorientation in the future. In so doing it will attempt to provide a clear description of the situation on either side of the Atlantic and to draw up recommendations for political action.

Initial paradoxes and asymmetries

The German-American relationship has never been easy to describe. In past decades it was characterized by a striking paradox: although regular and sometimes spectacular turbulence was to be observed on the surface, this was accompanied by a constant undercurrent of transatlantic friendship which was deeply rooted in public opinion and attitudes in general. Thus, for example, opinion polls in Germany and the USA have for decades revealed that Germans and Americans regularly put each other at the top of the list of specially favored nations. This was even the case during the Gulf War, at a time when criticism of America was rife in the German media. And the situation has not changed since the end of the East-West conflict. In a survey carried out in 1995 more than two thirds of all Germans stated that they were in favor of American troops remaining in Germany.

Despite this basically positive attitude, transatlantic dialogue has constantly been dominated by anxious discussion on the future of the partnership. Public opinion in Europe regularly speculates as to whether America really still has interests in Europe and whether American problems at home will not necessarily lead to a reduction in its foreign commitments.

Similarly, on the other side of the Atlantic, there is constant speculation as to whether Europe – which owes much of its greatness to the generous support given to it by America after the catastrophe of the Second World War – is now in a situation where it no longer needs America.

In contrast to the sometimes overly dramatic attitudes taken by intellectuals, the rhetoric of the politicians tends to overemphasize the actual degree of harmony, as though conflicts of interest, differences of opinion, arguments and irritations were not something that should ever occur within a friendship.

On closer scrutiny both these approaches – dramatization of differences and overemphasis of harmony – prove to be equally unrealistic. In many respects people on both sides of the Atlantic require a greater sense of proportion regarding the present situation and future prospects of the Euro-American relationship.

This tension between an overly dramatic and an overharmonizing approach to the transatlantic relationship is reflected in a number of paradoxes which crop up constantly in a variety of now classic variants:

- NATO links the Europeans and Americans within a security partnership, and yet for a wide variety of reasons, both partners regularly express their doubts as to the reliability of the other partner in security terms.
- The economies of Europe and America are closely interwoven in a network of investments and foreign trade, yet the two partners constantly accuse each other of infringing the rules of free world trade and pursuing their own advantage at the cost of the other.
- There have been many occasions on which the Euro-

peans have called on the Americans to demonstrate leadership. And yet as soon as the Americans start to do so, you can be sure that certain elements in European public opinion will begin to voice severe doubts. Conversely, since German unification America has ascribed a natural role of leader within Europe to the new Germany, but at the same time there are elements in American public opinion warning against an expanded and more powerful Germany.
- The Americans are constantly calling on the Europeans to finally take decisive action to further the European integration process. And yet in the past, as soon as this started to happen, critical voices were regularly raised in America claiming that such developments showed how Europe was increasingly turning its back on its transatlantic partner.

There is also a certain unmistakable lack of symmetry in the transatlantic relationship:

- Since the collapse of the Warsaw Pact, the USA has repeatedly demonstrated its role as a leading nation in global security policy, despite certain disasters and moments of indecision as, for example, in Haiti and Somalia. Since the disintegration of the Soviet Union, the USA has been the only credible source of order in the world. Compared with this, the European contribution, as was most recently demonstrated in Bosnia, has failed dramatically to meet the expectations attached to it.
- Despite the much-discussed symptoms of economic crisis, the USA remains the world's leading economy. European Economic and Monetary Union still only exists as an idea and has yet to prove itself in reality.

Despite episodes of chronic weakness, the dollar remains the world's leading currency. It remains to be
seen whether the new European currency will be
able to function at a similar level.
- A sense of political identity takes different forms on
either side of the Atlantic. While it is accepted as a
matter of course in America that the country should
offer an example to the rest of the world, Europe has
not yet reached the stage when it can make similar
claims for itself.

These asymmetries would be much more significant if
they were not tempered considerably by the fact that
the two continents have so many values and structures
in common, as well as by a long tradition of continuity
in Euro-American cooperation – continuity in the field
of security, continuity in constructive conflict-solving,
continuity in collaboration throughout the world within
the United Nations, the OSCE and in acute crisis situ-
ations – not to mention continuity with regard to close
economic and cultural cooperation.

So how do all these factors fit together? How are we
supposed to reconcile this mixture of misunderstand-
ings, sympathy and harsh criticism? How do we explain
this paradoxical mixture of closeness and alienation between Americans and Europeans? The answer will not
be found by looking at the headlines of the last few years
on Euro-American relations: burden sharing, protectionism, counterarmament debate, trade sanctions
against Iran, the lifting of the arms embargo in Bosnia.
Slogans like this symbolize a blinkered approach that is
limited to specific crises and therefore concentrates on
the superficial elements of a relationship. What is called
for, however, is an exploration of its depths.

The future of the western world and of Euro-American relations will not be decided by a specific issue, for example, a decision to order a specific type of weapon for NATO. Nor will it be decided by conflict arising from a particular economic disagreement. What will decide the future of the western world will be whether or not the political and cultural links across the Atlantic – links which created a "western world" in the first place – can be preserved and kept alive by future generations, even when external circumstances change. In view of the fact that the global political background against which the transatlantic alliance operates has changed radically since the upheavals of 1989, there is an urgent need to investigate the relationship anew.

Global political change requires a new quality of transatlantic relationship

Any attempt to redefine the future tasks of the Transatlantic Community first has to take into account the radical changes that have occurred in the global political scene since the early days of the relationship. Many of the figures and constellations in world politics that played a leading role in those days have lost their significance in recent years, and are no longer crucial for shaping strategies for the future and forming a new transatlantic leadership. Six major changes in the international political scene would seem to be of particular relevance:

1. The East-West conflict is no longer one of the main strategic determinants of world politics – and the dominating significance of security policy has also waned. The number of actors on the international political stage is growing, and with it the scope for different patterns of cooperation and conflict is also increasing. This development means that the power structures of old are having to be increasingly relativized. Although the USA has remained the only "superpower," it is finding it increasingly difficult to bring its weight to bear, because military and political domination is no longer as

crucial as it once was when it comes to solving the conflicts of the day (civil wars, economic crisis, nuclear
proliferation).

2. The traditional idea of national sovereignty is increasingly proving to be a utopian and naive relic of the
past. The vast majority of the problems and tasks facing
politicians today transcend national frontiers. But the
growing international nature of these problems is not
yet matched by any adequate political decision-making
structures. The result is that politicians are set to lose
their capacity to make decisions, little by little, unless
they can redevelop it in the form of effective international organizations.

3. In both Western and Eastern Europe, albeit at different levels, people are trying to find an adequate response to the pressure to modernize. With the Single
European Act and the goal of economic and monetary
union, Western Europe has set itself an ambitious program. When a single European currency is eventually
introduced, the process of moving from bilateral relations between individual European states and the USA
to multilateral Euro-American relations will have
moved on to a new plane.

4. In the context of Eastern European attempts to
respond to the pressure to modernize, attention is fo-
cused on three areas: differentiation, opening up, and
pluralization. Here, ideology has lost something of its
ability to provide answers and create cohesion. The
old, apparently incompatible, ideological clash between West and East is becoming less drastic – indeed
is losing its convincingness. For the first time in its

history, it may well be that Europe is on the threshold of unity.

Faced with this change, one of the tenets of western policy towards Germany over recent decades now has to prove that it is still relevant, namely that the Federal Republic of Germany links itself closely to its western partners via common institutions and practical policies and incorporates its political interests and economic and social potential into the western community, in return for which the western partners' acceptance of Germany as an equal partner within the transatlantic alliance is unequivocal and guarantees the country's external security.

5. There is a shift of emphasis occurring within Euro-American relations. The dissolution of the Warsaw Pact and the substantial reduction in the number of American troops stationed in Europe mean that the defense and security policy aspects of Euro-American relations are losing importance, while at the same time, economic and cultural aspects are looming larger. This brings with it a finer balance between the political and economic weights on either side of the Atlantic. Furthermore, the Americans are rediscovering their respect for the dynamism of the old continent. It will be in America's own interest to establish a presence in what may well become one of the strongest and most dynamic parts of the global market.

The Europe of the Fifteen is responsible for approximately one quarter of world economic production, even though it only accounts for some seven percent of the world's population. One third of world currency reserves are found in the European Community. And its share of world trade is almost 40 percent – more than the external trade volume of the USA and Russia put together. Thus the European Community is already the biggest trading partner in the world.

6. The spread of modern technology is drawing the world together to an extent hitherto unknown. The result is an increase in the impact of both regional conflicts and fundamentalist movements. The global network of information and mass media is giving rise to new forms of international debate. The subjective world of individuals' wishes, hopes and anxieties, this world of pictures and information, is increasingly forming a new central nerve of today's societies and holding the attention of the world's politicians.

All in all, one thing is clear: never before have so many changes occurred simultaneously in so many regions of the world. And these changes mean that a long, critical look needs to be taken at the reliability and solidity of traditional structures. The crucial element for the future architecture of transatlantic structures will remain the political will of all those involved.

For any new approach there has to be an awareness on both sides of the Atlantic of the possible reasons for continuing a Euro-American partnership. Are the – undeniably friendly – feelings for one another merely the result of a fifty-year experience with a common security policy – i.e. a defensive alliance – or are they based on a deeper sense of community that offers a more reliable foundation for a future relationship? And if the latter is the case, what elements of this feeling of communality can be activated in order to trigger off a new start that has some prospect of success?

The common elements –
a historically grown partnership

The early days of the Transatlantic Community

The Euro-American partnership does not just date from the Marshall Plan and the founding of NATO – it goes right back to the early years of the United States. Ever since settlers first arrived in North America and the USA came into being, there have been links between Europe and America unlike those between any other regions of the world.

America was born of the ideas of the European Enlightenment: rationality, human rights, freedom, equality, democracy. It was the progressive idealism of the Enlightenment that gave birth to the "American Dream." For many Europeans the decision to emigrate to America was an act of liberation from the oppressive constraints of Europe. In constructing America, the ideals of the Old World were used to create a better New World in which a wealth of ideas from the old continent would be realized more rapidly and more directly than was possible in a Europe frequently caught in the throes of bloody conflicts. In America, the brilliance and continuity of progressive idealism was able to develop in an atmosphere free from the European tendency to lapse into the ambivalence of dogmas and totalitarianism.

In addition to this contribution of European ideas to the founding of the New World, there were also other forms of exchange which are frequently overlooked. The practical foundations of American society – its legal and administrative system, religion and customs – were also imported from Europe, and as a result the Americans always regarded Europe as the continent where they had their roots and without which their own identity could not be properly understood.

Conversely, from the very beginning, America has played an important role in molding European ideas and politics. Goethe wrote a famous poem in which he congratulated the Americans for escaping the sad heritage of Europe's feudal structures. Of much greater political significance for European conditions was the prediction made by de Tocqueville in 1835, "that we, like the Americans, will sooner or later achieve almost complete equality." In other words, from a very early stage, America represented an ideal for the political classes in Europe. After the failed revolution of 1848, countless German democrats, who had been particularly inspired by the example of America, emigrated to the USA where they were able to implement their ideas successfully.

In the nineteenth century it was above all the lower classes, the ambitious middle classes and democrats in Europe who regarded America as the home of modernity, a country in which origins and class differences were no longer relevant, and every citizen could achieve economic and social success solely on the grounds of his or her own ability. And as early as the 1800s there were Europeans calling for US intervention to support democratic movements in Europe.

Even over and above political idealism, from the outset many Europeans were fascinated by the extraordinary dynamism of American society which succeeded in transcending the narrow geographical and social constraints of Europe. The idea of the "self-made man," the mobility of American society and the relative ease with which new approaches to old problems were found were regarded by generations of Europeans as an inspiration and a model to be emulated.

However, from the very beginning, there were also certain ambiguities in the relationship between Europe and America. America had come into being out of a need to distance itself from the old Europe. The new state made a conscious effort to dissociate itself from the traditional power games within Europe, with its constant military adventures in the service of feudal or absolutist regimes, its rigid class structures and religious intolerance. This was the light in which Americans viewed Europe. Right down to the time of the American Civil War the USA feared – with some justification – that the Europeans would use every opportunity to ensure that the "American experiment," which they disliked so much, would fail.

In cultural terms, the Americans initially felt extremely inferior to the Europeans, though at the same time Europeans tended to be regarded in the USA as arrogant and conceited. Many in Europe, on the other hand, complained about the unsophisticated, direct manner of the Americans – which they felt infringed the European rules, their lack of any social traditions and their largely materialistic approach to life.

Thus, from the very outset, America and Europe were aware not only of their differences but also of their mutual attraction and their interdependency. This dialectical tension lent the relationship between these two continents an intensity and dynamism in the early days which was to increase towards the end of the 19th century.

America's debut on the European political stage

In his inaugural speech as third President of the USA in 1801, Thomas Jefferson laid down the basic tenets of American foreign policy which have remained unchanged to this day: the USA was to avoid all foreign entanglements that could get it embroiled in the power struggles of other countries. But this never meant that the USA was going to abstain from active foreign policy. In their dealings with their former mother country, and later in their implementation of the Monroe Doctrine, especially against the European powers and in the expansion of American territory towards the West and South, American politicians in those early days displayed just as much cool calculation, diplomatic skill and determination as their contemporary counterparts in Europe.

The Americans quickly realized that the objectives of their foreign policy could only be achieved if they were able to influence the European states in a targeted manner. An early example of this was the Louisiana Purchase from Napoleon in 1803 for 15 million dollars, which displayed the skill with which American foreign policy was able to exploit the rivalries between France, England and Spain during that period.

Thus even in the last century America was never indifferent towards the turn of events in Europe. Its foreign policy could not simply be described in terms of isolationism, but is better seen as one of vigilant neutrality vis-à-vis the internal affairs of Europe.

Notwithstanding this political neutrality, social contacts across the Atlantic were already becoming close. American academics, particularly at elite universities such as Yale and Harvard, maintained close contacts with their European partners. Tens of thousands of American students were already attending British – and above all German – universities during the 19th century. The European ideal of education, and the British example in particular, dominated the ideas of the upper classes in America. And economic relations between Europe and America were from the very outset based on close mutual dependence.

By the end of the 19th century, increasing world-wide economic and social interdependence, together with the exponential growth in America's economic strength, had reached such a level that America began to regard political intervention in the global arena as increasingly necessary. At this stage, American economic performance was already stronger than that of every single European nation. At the turn of the century the USA was, for example, producing five times as much steel as Great Britain, and American wheat exports were becoming an increasing problem for Europe, in particular for German producers. Europe tried to defend itself by introducing customs barriers. The USA responded by proclaiming to the world its policy of "open doors" – i.e. free trade.

Thus, action on the world stage, as far as the USA was concerned, was primarily a matter of tackling the traditional European powers, which were expanding globally during the age of imperialism. For their part, the European states regarded the increasing economic and political power of America as the first step towards that country's involvement in world politics, and renewed their efforts to get the USA on their side. They were particularly keen to use the USA as a counterbalance to their rivals in Europe – and thus also as a balancing factor within the old continent.

In other words, the years between 1890 and 1917, when America entered the First World War, saw the USA becoming inexorably involved in European politics – even if this was a process with certain interruptions.

In 1898 the USA became involved in its first war on overseas territory (the Philippines), i.e. outside the area of application of the Monroe Doctrine, and against a European nation (Spain). In 1900 American troops were sent overseas for the first time to participate in the international contingent sent to deal with the Boxer Rebellion in Peking. Later, in 1906, the American President actively intervened to achieve a peaceful solution of the Moroccan crisis – the first example of American mediation in a region that had traditionally been part of the European sphere of influence.

At this stage the question on behalf of which side the USA would intervene in Europe had already been answered. Since 1895, Britain had been working determinedly to create a strategic alliance with the USA – and in doing so had displayed considerable willingness to compromise. One of the main factors that persuaded the Americans to side with the British and the *Entente* was a fear of a total German domination of Europe – i.e. traditional considerations related to maintaining a balance of power in Europe.

But there was another new criterion which, to this day, has remained a central element of American policy: involvement in war in Europe purely in order to maintain the balance of power would have infringed Jefferson's principle of avoiding "foreign entanglements." The American public, moreover, regarded such an approach as too defensive and incompatible with the history of the New World. America had largely come into being on the basis of the "American Dream" of universal freedom and equality. The USA did not traditionally feel obliged to export its model, but from the very start laid claim to being a worldwide beacon for the new ideas of the Enlightenment.

Thus, President Wilson's main argument in favor of entering the First World War and becoming involved in European politics, was not that American economic or political interests were under threat, but rather that the basic values of the "American Dream" of freedom and self-determination were endangered in the very continent from which they had first emerged and which had always been closely linked to the USA.

Seen from this perspective, the natural ally for America in Europe was the liberal-democratic social system in Britain, which was perceived as being locked into a struggle for survival against the autocratic, expansionist state of Germany. It was only by reinterpreting a war that had emerged from the traditional approach to power politics as a conflict over the realization of basic democratic values that American politicians were able to justify US involvement in this war to the American public.

Of course, such a reinterpretation also meant a re-modelling. America was not pursuing the traditional objectives of its allies, who were mainly interested in a redistribution of power within Europe. The USA – as Wilson formulated it – was fighting "for the universal application of law within the concert of free peoples, for security and peace for all nations." In other words: America was prepared to guarantee the security of the free nations of Europe with its own military might, provided the Europeans responded by giving up their traditional warlike diplomacy based on undemocratic decisions and developing amongst themselves and in cooperation with America a community based on democratic values.

Underlying this political concept was the American belief that, in a world liberated from state control of the economic and social spheres, American interests would prevail "naturally" within a system of unrestrained competition.

This aim has remained the basis of American policy on Europe during the entire course of this century and, in the wake of the Second World War, was the crucial precondition for the setting up of NATO as well as the EEC. Thus, America played a crucial role in ensuring that the originally European ideas of freedom, equality and self-determination, which eighty years ago were still regarded as an alien element in international relations, have prevailed as the basic principles of foreign policy, at least in Western Europe.

The lessons of the inter-war period – Europe and America in the twenties and thirties

The vision of an increasing integration of democratic nations was to suffer a severe setback following the First World War. The American Congress vetoed the USA's accession to the organization that was regarded as the central instrument for creating a new world order – the League of Nations – even though its approach and organization were strongly influenced by American ideas. Without the involvement of what was by now the world's leading country in both economic and political terms, this model of a universal body for the maintenance of peace was doomed to failure.

The ripples caused by this withdrawal of America from Europe are still being felt to this day, and on both sides of the Atlantic even trivial differences between Europeans and Americans result in the continued danger of American isolationism being invoked.

What tends to be forgotten is the fact that, despite a temporary drop in the intensity of political cooperation between Europe and the USA during the inter-war period, the social, cultural – and above all the economic – links across the Atlantic continued to increase. And even in the political sphere contacts remained extremely active.

At an early stage, the Americans took on a leading role in the task of economic reconstruction in Europe. Aware of the high level of economic interdependency, US economic experts quickly realized that a rapid recovery from the recession which the war had caused in Europe would be an important element in ensuring the health of the American economy. Unlike France and Britain, the USA endeavored to put Germany in a position where it could fulfill its duties under the Treaty of Versailles regarding reparations payments. The Americans were convinced that, without economic stabilization in Germany, peace would not return to Europe. Thus, a leading role in regulating the financial structures for European reconstruction was played by American bankers like Charles Dawes and Owen Young, using American capital and having the support of the American government. This meant, amongst other things, that even at this stage the dollar also started to assume the role of reserve currency in Europe.

In political terms, too, the US government was extremely active in Europe during this period, and made full use of its increased influence. The principle of most-favored nation status, i.e. liberalization of trade, was further expanded in Europe. And behind the scenes, American diplomats were working feverishly to obtain a peaceful settlement within Europe. In addition, America launched new initiatives in the sphere of disarmament (including the Briand-Kellog Pact of 1928 renouncing war). By now America was an integral part of the European political scene.

At the same time, the twenties and thirties witnessed a process of social change which has continued right up to the present day: America started to dominate European mass culture both materially and in terms of content. Hollywood movies conquered Europe, while the American entertainment industry, American music and American dances began to spread throughout the world. Europe was flooded with American consumer goods, which set new standards for European products too. By the mid-twenties the USA had become the world's greatest exporting nation, and the Americans increasingly began to see themselves as the one and only source of modern ideas – especially for Europe.

In the thirties, the world economic crisis led to a temporary slowing in the growth of the Euro-American relationship. The economic and financial order painstakingly built up with American help during the twenties collapsed and was replaced by a renationalization of monetary and economic policy which also spread to other areas of political life.

It became clear that a policy of involvement without commitment as pursued by the Europeans and Americans in the period following the First World War did not offer an adequate basis for a lasting transatlantic relationship. Despite close social links and a broad range of political contacts and joint projects, the Europeans and Americans did not have the strength to resist the centrifugal forces resulting from the collapse of the Versailles order.

It would, however, be wrong to attach all the blame for this failure to the USA and to ascribe it to American reluctance to assume a leading role within Europe. At the time the European states regarded possible American dominance in Europe with the utmost suspicion. They did not, as yet, have any experience with international financial institutions. And as the international economic crisis deepened, the Europeans too, were dominated by a tendency to cut themselves off from the outside world. There was a general fear that excessively close and open cooperation with the USA would lead to the crisis being solved at Europe's expense.

The underlying reason for the crisis at that time was not the way the USA apparently turned its back on Europe. The establishment of a new order in Europe failed because neither the European states nor the USA were yet ready for the vision, put forward by the USA after the First World War, of a transatlantic (and, ideally, world-wide) community of democratic states that would renounce military rivalries once and for all and agree on credible guarantees for their common security.

Building the Transatlantic Community after the Second World War

Thus, when the states of Europe and the USA came to tackle the question of restructuring the transatlantic relationship following the Second World War, they were able to look back on a rich and varied history of joint policies and mutual dependency. On both sides of the Atlantic there was a firm belief that strategies for solving international problems only had a prospect of succeeding if they were based on cooperation with the transatlantic partner(s). The vision of a community of states based on democratic principles had appeared on the horizon, but proof was still outstanding that this was feasible in reality.

The fact that the idea had fallen on fertile ground was demonstrated at an early stage after the National Socialists launched their war in Europe. Building on its experience during the First World War, and taking up President Wilson's concept of universal peace, the USA seized the initiative and, in 1941, formulated the Atlantic Charter together with Britain. This document not only records the will of the democratic nations to resist German aggression but also, in principle, opens up a vision similar to the American vision back in 1917: the creation of a free order based on the self-determination of nations, a secure peace and a liberal, non-discriminatory world trade system.

In 1945, unlike in 1918, steps were taken to realize this vision. There were two factors which crucially influenced this new approach: firstly, the appalling destruction and atrocities of the Second World War demonstrated that the traditional European policy of maintaining a balance of power was both practically and morally defunct. And secondly, the growing Soviet threat which emerged soon after the end of the war brought home to the states of the Western world the urgency of developing a genuinely common defense and security policy.

Nevertheless, the decision to set up the western alliance had to be implemented by the fathers of the post-war order such as George Marshall, Robert Schuman and Konrad Adenauer against sometimes considerable resistance both internally and externally. In Germany the idea of irreversible incorporation into the western alliance was controversial because this could be interpreted as a permanent relinquishment of the possibility of unification. And in other western European states this irreversible linking with the USA also drew criticism, as did the de facto admission of the recent enemy, Germany, to the new peace order on equal terms. And in the USA such permanent and binding guarantees of security for Europe were also a novel idea – and as such controversial.

Given the situation at the time, the setting up of the western alliance – primarily NATO, but also its economic counterpart, the EEC – was thus by no means a process that could be taken for granted. It is only thanks to the subsequent success of these new structures that we today regard them as having been the only logical consequence of the Second World War. Ultimately the credit for creating this new order has to go to the vision, determination and practical skills displayed by the post-war generation of politicians, who recognized and grasped the only chance for making a new start and ensured its success through their domestic and foreign policies.

The most far-reaching consequences of this reorientation were undoubtedly felt in German foreign policy. The Federal Republic of Germany had to completely reposition the basic coordinates of its policy – dropping the uncertainties of having to define its position on every issue, relinquishing all go-it-alones and nationalistic policies, and making a clear commitment to cooperation on the stabilization of western freedoms. Thus, for the first time ever, the country's internal order and external alignment matched each other. Political culture had become the compass with which the Germans in the Federal Republic mapped their position within the world. And this position was and indeed remains one of integration, a concept covering many things – incorporation into the western alliance, German-American friendship and European unity.

The links thus created between Germany and America, some of which were based on formal treaties, meant that the Federal Republic had definitively invested all its interests and its potential into the common Western strategy. And the states of the West, led by the Americans, also committed themselves to taking German interests into consideration in all matters – including the German Question.

The role played by the Americans in the historic task of rebuilding Western Europe after the Second World War went far beyond the mere supplying of material investment. America gave the defeated in Europe an opportunity to regain their self-respect – and earned gratitude in return. But anyone who invests so much non-material commitment inevitably becomes more susceptible to apparent irritations – for example when yesterday's protégé begins to assert itself, or when support for European unity not only reduces political tensions but also creates first and foremost an economic competitor – or when in the eyes of many Germans their much-admired role model excessively indulges in a kind of "world-power-tactics."

The stations of the alliance – from overemphasis of the positive to mature cooperation

Even after the establishment of the post-war order, the development of the transatlantic alliance did not always run smoothly and was not always free of internal conflicts. Initially, the main focus was on trying out and ensuring the continued existence, particularly internally, of a hitherto virtually unknown level of cooperation. Just how difficult this was in some instances can be seen from the German debate on rearmament and NATO membership. In addition to this, the balance vis-à-vis the Warsaw Pact was by no means as stable as it was to become in the sixties and seventies, when the policy of "peaceful coexistence" was accepted on all sides.

Thus in the 1950s, there was a tendency on both sides of the Atlantic to overemphazise the positive elements in the relationship. Particularly in the Federal Republic of Germany, the USA was regarded as the ultimate role model. A tendency to imitate took over, and this was underpinned by a shared antipathy towards Communism. On the other side of the Atlantic, Europe, after implementation of the Marshall Plan, was regarded as a result of realization of the "American Dream." America was using its dynamic economic strength and passionately held belief in the idea of a free, democratic and modern society to assist at the rebirth of a new American-style Europe.

During these years the Federal Republic of Germany, in particular, was regarded as a sort of miniature USA. Just as the American public regarded the GDR as "Russian Germany," so, too, the Federal Republic was seen as the "good, American" Germany, in other words "our Germany." The restoration of democracy was seen as a reimportation of the ideas of the European Enlightenment from the USA. The successful combination of stable democracy and high levels of economic growth meant that America regarded its German partner as the product of American ideals.

The second stage in German-American post-war relations started at the end of the sixties. This stage was characterized by an overemphasis of the negative aspects. In cultural terms, many people now started to regard the USA as the epitome of everything that was negative and despicable. Vietnam was a symbol of bloodthirsty aggression, Watergate a symbol of political corruption, the fast food temples and soap operas an indication that any aspiration to cultural standards had long since been abandoned. These were the stock perceptions of America amongst European intellectuals.

This change of attitude was helped by an increasing self-confidence amongst Europeans. But at the same time this loss of a role model triggered a debate amongst Europeans about their real identity – particularly in Germany, which had traditionally been America's most loyal ally.

It was no longer possible to answer questions like "Who are we?" or "How would we like to be?" simply by saying "Like the Americans." This increasing tendency for the Germans to seek their own identity was also reflected by a change of attitude on the other side of the Atlantic. Many people over there began to regard the Germans as unreliable partners who were beginning to flirt with the old dream of finding an independent role between East and West.

The third period then started with the eighties and brought a more balanced assessment of both the positive and negative elements. The USA was now neither glorified nor vilified in Europe. A sober realization of the scope and limitations facing transatlantic cooperation began to characterize the mutual assessment of each other. There was a greater awareness both of shared interests and of differences.

The collapse of the Warsaw Pact and the new challenges which this brought merely served to further strengthen this tendency towards a sober assessment of transatlantic relations. The disintegration of the former enemy was not celebrated as a triumph, but rather seen as a moment to make an immediate start on the task of political and economic reconstruction in the eastern part of a continent which for so long had been divided. The fact that the interests of the individual partners within the western alliance were by no means identical was a further reason to adopt a sober approach.

Thus the process of German unification would by far probably not have been as rapid or as cooperative if the Americans had not supported it so actively, even in the face of doubts on the part of their Western European partners. Different degrees of emphasis also emerged in attitudes towards Russia, the sharing out of the burden of economic reconstruction in Eastern Europe, and – particularly strikingly – over the crisis in the former Yugoslavia precipitated by the collapse of the Eastern bloc.

On the other hand, many classic differences within

the alliance disappeared completely, such as the debate on the instruments required for a common security policy and the controversy which had raged during the eighties about upgrading medium and short-range missiles. And the regular protests against the stationing of American troops in various states in Europe also disappeared. Even the debate about burden sharing within security policy seems nowadays to have lost its urgency.

Instead of these issues, transatlantic political attention is now focusing on those controversies that were regarded as of secondary importance in the past – in particular differing reactions to crises in third countries including nuclear proliferation, the combating of international terrorism, and also the regularly occurring transatlantic trade wars.

In addition, the disintegration of the Warsaw Pact and the disappearance of the immediate security threat meant that both Europe and the USA began to concentrate to a much greater degree than ever before on their own domestic problems. The EU faces the twin challenges of deepening the Community at Maastricht II and carrying out the enlargement to the east which it has promised the reform states of Central and Eastern Europe. In the USA, Clinton's electoral success in 1992 and the triumph of the Republicans in the congressional elections of 1994 meant that the political agenda has been increasingly dominated by problems of domestic policy – most recently to the exclusion of all other issues.

Thus, before one can assess the scope for a new start in transatlantic relations following the upheavals of 1989–1991, it is necessary to take a look at the present domestic situation of the partners involved. To what extent, given their domestic political agenda, will Europe and America be in a position to jointly assume international responsibilities? What kind of transatlantic relationship will the public on either side of the Atlantic be prepared to accept, now that the immediate security threat is fading?

The USA on the threshold of the 21st century – a turning point in domestic affairs

Immediately following its victory in the Gulf War in 1991, all the indications were that the USA, boosted by its moral and military triumph, would devote itself with some energy to building up the "New World Order" which had been proclaimed by President Bush. But America's enjoyment of its victory turned out to be short-lived. Clinton's success in the presidential elections of 1992, followed by the Republicans' landslide victory in the Congressional elections of 1994, meant that American politics started to move in an entirely different direction. The country now had to start tackling the domestic problems which, after decades of neglect, had grown to massive proportions.

Economic and social problems

In 1988, during the election campaign, there had already been the first rumblings of concern – initiated by the then presidential candidate, Dukakis – and by 1992, it was obvious that important elements in American public opinion had a very clear idea of the exceedingly serious social and economic problems that had to be solved at home.

America is now engaged in a debate which is unprecedented in its sheer breadth – a dialogue which, albeit superficially, contrasts strangely with the carefully celebrated restoration of American self-confidence vis-à-vis the outside world which had taken place under Presidents Reagan and Bush.

In essence there are two main problem areas:

1. The greatest concern is clearly related to the state of the economy. Here the overriding problem is the US federal budget deficit, which is running out of control and, moreover, appears to have become a permanent structural problem.

Even the plan carefully negotiated between Congress and the administration in 1990, to reduce the predicted deficit by 500 billion dollars by 1995, has clearly failed – despite the fact that the budget figures for 1994 and 1995 (deficits of 204 and 164 billion dollars respectively), represent an improvement of some 25 percent compared with 1990. The total federal debt has grown from 3,000 billion dollars in 1991 to a current figure of almost 5,000 billion dollars. Each year, approximately 300 billion dollars interest for these debts has to be paid from the federal budget. This makes up nearly 20 percent of the entire annual expenditure of the American Federal Government. The conflict over this issue has increased dramatically since the Republicans gained a majority in Congress in January 1995.

The problem of the budget deficit is made worse by the extremely low level of savings in the USA. On average only five percent of disposable income is saved, whereas the figures for Germany and Japan are twelve percent and 15 percent respectively. Thus the deficit in the USA has to be financed from foreign sources to a much greater degree than in Europe. This has led to a situation whereby, in the space of a few years, the USA has moved from being the world's biggest creditor country to being the biggest debtor country. Internationally, it is some 650 billion dollars in the red.

However, the budget deficit is by no means the only economic problem facing the USA. The average annual rise in productivity in the American economy over the last ten years was a mere 1.1 percent. America's technological lead, which in the eyes of the Americans is the crucial factor underlying the country's leading role in the world, has disappeared completely in many areas and been noticeably reduced in others.

As a result of this development America no longer produces any colour television sets, for example. And many other products are now being produced better and more cheaply abroad. This, in turn, is an explanation for the chronic American balance of trade deficit, which has again reached record levels during the past two years. This gloomy picture is completed by inadequate investment levels, which are running at some 50 percent of those in Japan and clearly below of those in most other important Western industrial states. During the last years of the Clinton administration, though, some indicators have improved for a short time. High growth rates have again been noted for the gross domestic product, unemployment has decreased, and the big companies have, in particular, again strengthened their productivity and competitive position by drastic rationalization. This economic upturn has, however, not fundamentally changed the structural economic problems such as deficit financing, neglect of the infrastructure and insufficient savings and investment rates. The Americans are, quite simply, consuming too much and neglecting the necessary renewal of the country's infrastructure and productive capacity.

2. Clearly linked to the state of the economy are short-comings in social integration – though many Americans no longer take these as seriously as the economic problems.

Increasing numbers of Americans are simply missing out on the "American Dream." Some 37 million, i.e. 14.7 percent of the entire population are officially classed as "poor." More than three million of these Americans living below the poverty level are working full-time. The phenomenon of the "working poor" has become a sad peculiarity of the American social debate. Moreover, 37 million have no form of medical insurance whatsoever. Between 1980 and 1992, during a period of unusually high economic growth, the average hourly wage of American industrial workers actually fell by eight percent, and between 1973 and 1989 the hourly wage of 25 to 34-year-old men without a university education declined by as much as 18.3 percent.

In areas inhabited by the lower social classes, conditions – whether you measure these in terms of basic socio-economic data or of the infrastructure of daily life – are becoming increasingly akin to those in Third World countries. A recent survey revealed that black people living in the Bronx in New York have a shorter life expectancy than inhabitants of Bangladesh. In general terms it has been demonstrated that even though open – sometimes legally sanctioned – discrimination of blacks and other minorities has virtually disappeared, the achievement of true social equality is still light years away.

A particularly severe problem is posed by increasingly evident shortcomings in the education system, which contribute to the growing marginalization of large sections of the population. At its best, the American education system leads the world. But a concentration on excellence at the top end has led to an increasing neglect of education and training for the broad masses. Comparative studies indicate that the Americans lag woefully behind in terms of general knowledge. In California, for example, 4.5 million of the 29 million inhabitants are illiterate, and 25 percent of school leavers have no formal qualifications whatsoever.

Faced with this depressing situation it is not surprising that many Americans perceive their country's position in the world as being under threat. Of course, there are also those amongst the public who regard any debate about an American crisis as the talk of defeatist "liberals." They follow President F.D. Roosevelt's dictum that "We have nothing to fear but fear itself" and regard warnings about the imminent decline of America as constituting the only danger in sight.

This school of thought does not deny outright that there is a need to tackle shortcomings in one field or another. However, it refuses to admit that the problems now facing America differ in terms of quality from the challenges of days gone by.

The theory of America's decline

At the other end of the spectrum are the "declinists," who regard America – like other major powers in the past – as condemned to undergo a largely unavoidable process of decline which at best can only be cushioned in social terms (Paul Kennedy). America, they believe, has overstretched itself in its foreign policy, largely through its worldwide military presence, but also through its expenditure on development and economic aid. Thus the money that could have contributed to economic renewal at home has been wasted elsewhere. The conclusion they draw is that the USA must drastically reduce, above all, its military spending and its foreign financial commitments.

However, this theory that the present state of the USA is due to the country having overstretched itself abroad does not stand up to close scrutiny. For a start, it is not supported by the facts. Despite its considerable expenditure on defense technology during the eighties, America has never spent more than six percent of its gross national product on the military.

This percentage may be higher than the equivalent figure for the (old) Federal Republic of Germany (four percent), but not by such a large margin that it could have resulted in the economic consequences painted in such lurid terms by the "declinists." And in the sphere of public development aid the USA actually occupies one of the bottom places amongst western countries, only spending 0.21 percent of GNP on development aid, whereas Germany spends 0.39 percent. Furthermore, what the "declinists" also fail to include in their calculations are the advantages resulting from their country's foreign involvements.

It is perhaps significant that Kennedy's theories have met with a largely critical reception amongst American academics and enjoy relatively little support today. But they are indicative of a certain political position, and reflect very accurately a rather vague but dominant belief found amongst the US public at large, which is combined with other elements, such as demands for trade sanctions against trading partners who are supposedly cheating America. A further role may also be played by the fact that the Americans are no more able than any other nation to resist the temptation to blame their own problems on "foreigners" – and "declinism" is the perfect solution to this need for a scapegoat.

These "declinism" theories are particularly dangerous because they fail to recognize the true nature of foreign relations – a failure which has a long tradition in America. In stark contrast to the European states, America is much more wrapped up in its own affairs. The sheer size of the country means that, in many respects, it is self-sufficient. In a Europe divided into nation states, the maintenance of an active foreign policy has been in a very real sense a matter of sheer survival – whereas it has always been regarded as somewhat of an unnecessary luxury in America.

This can be the only explanation why the American public views expenditure on foreign and international policy purely as a drain on resources – and for the same reason tends to regard its own foreign policy largely as an expression of moral duty.

This attitude even makes sense if one accepts the basic premise that if action does not result from functionalist – i.e. egoistic – motives, then it can only be interpreted as being an altruistic realization of foreign interests. The American presence in Europe, for example, then becomes a case of the strong selflessly providing help for the weak. As every visitor to the USA confirms time and time again, any attempt to suggest to Americans that they are serving their own interests by maintaining a presence in Europe is met with incomprehension.

But because some recipients of American generosity now appear to be outstripping their benefactor, it is easy to perceive the success of such rivals as being the other side of the same coin and to blame America's problems on their success.

This attempt to explain America's problems in terms of foreign policy does not only ignore the objective facts of the situation. Worse still, the conclusions drawn by apologists of this theory actually serve to draw America further into this mire of misconception. Nowadays, the USA cannot exist as an "Isle of the Blessed" any more than any other country. In a shrinking and increasingly interdependent world in which everyone is affected by everything that happens, even the USA is an integral part of one global economy.

Nothing demonstrates this more clearly than the USA's "double deficit" (trade and budget). This relativizes the threat posed by many other developments. Even America has to bow to the economic law of comparative costs. If other countries can produce higher quality goods at a lower cost, this also increases prosperity in America – provided America can pay for these goods with its own exports, not by borrowing. Thus the correct action to take would be to concentrate more on the world market rather than shutting oneself off from it.

The criticisms voiced by the prophets of doom also lack a sense of proportion. It cannot be denied, for example, that the American share of global GNP (a favorite statistic quoted by the "declinists") has dropped significantly since the end of the Second World War. In 1946 it was between 40 percent and 45 percent, whereas by 1991 it had declined to 23 percent. But this can easily be explained in terms of the unusual situation at the time: all economic powers of any importance, apart from the USA itself, had suffered severe – even devastating – damage during the war. Since the world's recovery from the impact of war, the US share of global GNP has actually remained constant at 22 percent to 23 percent. It is also correct to say that America still turns in an economic performance which, in volume, is about twice that of its closest rival, Japan. This reflects more or less accurately the size of the populations of the two countries.

Nor is it enough to look at economic criteria alone. Not only is the USA the world's leading military state – and set to remain so for the foreseeable future – it is also (notwithstanding European arrogance in this regard) a first-class cultural power as well. The leading position of the USA is indicated, for example, by its complete domination of the movie industry, without doubt *the* art form of the 20th century. All this is enough to demonstrate that for the foreseeable future at least, America, even if its role is continually reduced, will continue to be in an excellent position.

The "worst case scenario" would be that the USA's lead over its rivals might be cut back somewhat. Europe may catch up – but will never move ahead.

To say this is not to deny that the USA faces severe problems. However, does not this surely indicate that the problems concerned require nothing more than the sort of adjustment to new developments the likes of which every state has to carry out on a routine basis? Will it be enough, though, for America simply to give full rein to the American virtues? This assumption is countered by the fact that this present crisis appears to have one unique characteristic, namely it is none other than the traditional problem-solving approach offered by American political culture that is proving insufficient.

It would seem obvious that in the field of social policy one significant source of problems is quite simply the unwillingness of American taxpayers to come up with the necessary revenue. The average American taxpayer pays 25 percent in taxes, whereas the equivalent figure for Britain is 37 percent, France 38 percent and the Federal Republic of Germany 39 percent.

And this is where one crucial problem lies. Historically speaking, the USA is the home of liberalism – in the old sense of the word. The country was born of tax rebellion (the Boston Tea Party) and defined from the very outset by an attempt to keep the state out of the lives of its citizens in as many areas as possible. Underlying this approach is the assumption that the citizen is always in a better position to solve his problems than the state. By way of contrast, conservatism and social democracy – the two most important schools of political thought in Europe – both require a strong state, albeit for different reasons.

Nevertheless, in recent years there have been recurring calls even in the USA for state intervention to solve the urgent economic and social problems facing the country. Thus President Clinton's – now failed – government program to reform the health system and social insurance, schools and the vocational training system, was the first direct attempt to deal with these problem areas through comprehensive state involvement. The theoretical sources on which the program was based include a book written by the present American Secretary of Labor, Robert Reich, entitled "The Work of Nations," in which the author states that high quality school education for all is by far the most important foundation stone for economic success. However, the American public has not, as yet, displayed any inclination to support the necessary government intervention, and this is also the reason for the program's failure following its rejection, for the time being, by the US Congress in 1994.

President Clinton's initiatives – widely regarded as too radical by the American people – have now even resulted in public opinion swinging in the opposite direction. The new Republican majority in Congress believes that less state support for the weaker elements in society will strengthen their initiative and lead them out of poverty. A broad political front has emerged that now supports reduced social security payments and lower taxes for the average citizen. Proof that this would actually enable the poorer elements in society to improve their position has not yet been forthcoming. And such expectations are particularly unrealistic, as similarly, the retraining and vocational programs required do not fit into the picture of a state-free economy.

It is quite clear that basic rights are viewed merely as being the rights of the citizens to defend themselves against the state. In sharp contrast to the European approach, basic rights in America lack a social dimension. In Europe, guaranteeing such rights is viewed as the task of the state both by Christian social teaching and socialist and social-democratic theories.

If, therefore, this basic American view that the individual has to be freed from a nanny state and stand on his own two feet is incapable of solving the country's present problems, it might seem obvious to recommend to the Americans that they look abroad, or more specifically to Europe. While it is true that the cost of social security systems has posed an enormous burden on the public purse in European states, it has at least ensured that conditions such as those found in the Bronx do not prevail anywhere in Europe.

It would, of course, be naive and unrealistic simply to offer the Americans a copy of European solutions, but a degree of mutual interchange on social matters would fit into the picture of a world characterized by increasing interdependence – and would help reduce social costs on both sides of the Atlantic. Europe, too, could learn a lot from America, including how to mobilize academic excellence, how to organize the university system, and generally how to cope with social change. It would thus be to the advantage of both partners if the necessary structures for such a mutual learning process could be set up.

The new ethnic composition of America –
is Europe set to disappear?

Will Europe and the European origins of so many Americans continue to play the same role in the future as they have in the past? The most recent American census in 1990 revealed an impressive picture of the latest demographic developments in the USA. Of the 248.7 million people living in the USA in that year, 19.7 million were born outside the country – a higher number than ever before in American history.

Of these, 4.4 million alone came from Mexico, and 5.4 million from Asia. Almost 32 million – a figure which must include at least twelve million people actually born in the USA – claimed to speak a language other than English at home. Of these, 17.3 million spoke Spanish, and 5.4 million an Asian language.

Without doubt, the 1980s saw a dynamic period of immigration, with more than seven million people flooding into the USA. And this is a trend which is set to continue: many experts predict the arrival of a further 15 million immigrants during the 1990s. California, with 30 million inhabitants the biggest American state, and together with Texas and Florida the one which is most affected by immigration, is set to lose its white majority by the turn of the century. This is a clear indication that the vast majority of the new immigrants are not of European origin. Is, therefore, the USA set to change in cultural terms? Is Europe in danger of sinking beneath the horizon, as those with ethnic links with Europe become a minority?

Even those immigrants who more or less accept most aspects of the American way of life will usually retain a certain loyalty towards their "homeland." This may be based largely on sentimentality, but can nevertheless sometimes significantly influence their actions. It could therefore be expected that an American identity that incorporates the original homeland would give rise to a wish amongst recent immigrants that the USA take into account the concerns of their country of origin in its foreign policy.

There are impressive examples of this to be found in American history, the most significant being the strong influence of the Jewish population which, in the decades following the Six-Day War, succeeded in ensuring that there was a close alliance between America and Israel.

But there are also plenty of counterexamples to be found, particularly amongst Americans of German origin. These form the largest of the identifiable ethnic minorities, but have never been able to exert any significant influence on American foreign policy – and indeed did not wish to do so after 1914.

The rise of East Asia – so far only in economic terms

– is undoubtedly a development of the utmost global significance which the USA and indeed every state with worldwide interests should take note of. This would be the only reason for America to concern itself more closely with developments in this region – it would certainly not do so because of immigration to the USA from the region.

Anyone who emigrates to the USA does so because the country's attractions per se make it more attractive than the social realities of that person's homeland. Nevertheless, this does not exclude the possibility of that person using his or her experience gained back home to work for changes in some aspects of life in the USA.

However, it is significant that the present ethnic shifts occurring in America are taking place against the background of an extremely passionate debate about a – real or imagined – "Eurocentrism" in America. The actual demographic changes seem to be being shadowed by rapid corresponding shifts in American identity.

Those who criticize American Eurocentrism claim that the American identity is excessively based on European models, that interpretations of history always take an exclusively European point of view, and that the contribution made by Americans of non-European origin to the building of America is ignored.

It is therefore logical that the debate on Eurocentrism should be accompanied by a comprehensive process of historical revisionism. The considerable cultural implications of this came out clearly during the Columbus anniversary year. For centuries the European conquest of America triggered by Columbus's discovery of that continent was regarded as part and parcel of the inevitable advance of progress in the world. The result was that the original Indian population became victims of an attitude based on social Darwinism and were dismissed as history's losers. Now the debate on Eurocentrism has opened the way for a diametrically opposed interpretation.

The pre-Columbian culture of America is increasingly being associated with an almost utopian perfection. The turning point in this development came with Kirkpatrick Sale's study "The Lost Paradise," in which the author explicitly emphasized that he did not wish the term "paradise" to be taken as a mere metaphor, but rather as a literal description of the Indian way of life at the time of the Europeans' arrival.

For a Europe which was going through a profound crisis at the end of the Middle Ages, America offered an opportunity for recovery which was, however, destroyed by Europeans driven by primitive material greed. This interpretation brings us back to Rousseau's "Noble Savage" – and the opening up of America becomes the white man's greatest sin. At the same time, the circle is completed and we return to the point of departure, one form of ethnocentrism merely having been replaced by another, this time non-European.

The practical implications of this realignment emerged first of all in the field of educational policy. Major American universities, as well as the state bodies responsible for drawing up curricula, have started to review the traditional educational canon. European history and literature have begun to be replaced by a greater focus on the Third World.

Seen from the point of view of Europe, this is nothing less than an attempt to eradicate – or at least to weaken – America's European roots. And yet to claim that this development is aimed against Europe would be to miss the point.

To illustrate this, it is necessary to put the Eurocentrism debate into a wider historical context. The patriotism that sustained the American people during the hard struggle for survival against the English colonialists in the 18th century and ultimately led to American independence could be described as "constitutional patriotism." The United States wanted to be different from the old Europe.

But one should also not forget that this was the self-same America which, in the early days, perceived itself as being English in cultural terms – and indeed was overwhelmingly English. America may never have been a nation state along European lines, but American identity – and here there is a strong parallelism with the states of Europe – was essentially rooted in a sense of belonging to a homogeneous nation in terms of such objective characteristics as language, origins, religion and lifestyle.

Thus, right from the early days of independence, America's identity was ambivalent. The strong pressure towards homogeneity during the revolution was initially weakened thereafter. The massive wave of immigrants from other European states that entered the country during the first half of the 19th century, above all from Ireland and Germany, met with considerable resistance on the grounds that such "un-English" immigrants would not be capable of integration.

The other possible approach to establishing an identity – the attempt to define Americanism both subjectively and societally in terms of common values – was, for long periods of American history, only attempted half-heartedly. The liberation of the black slaves, born of this desire to apply certain basic values to everyone in society, ground to a halt after the Civil War. Right up till the civil rights movement in the 1950s, the blacks were fobbed off with the slogan "equal but separate" – itself an expression of the desire to preserve ethnic identity.

There were two developments that gradually succeeded in weaning the Americans away from their ethnic identity during the course of the 20th century. The first was the First World War, which forced people to return their minds to the original values on which American society was based – for how otherwise could one have justified waging war against the Germans, who now made up a significant proportion of the American population? In addition, the challenges posed by the USA's confrontation with the totalitarian National Socialist and Communist regimes encouraged the development of a counterprogram.

On the other hand, a new wave of immigration hit America just prior to the turn of the century – this time from Italy, Austria-Hungary and Russia. The ethnic identity of America, which hitherto had been determined by the Western Europeans, now took in the whole of Europe. Thus the universalist tendency contained within the idea of human rights was reflected in a universalization of the ethnic composition of the country.

Seen in these terms, the mass immigration from non-European countries is merely the logical continuation of this development. The United States is now really becoming a "nation of nations," transcending any idea of ethnic identity.

What America now has to do is to avoid the danger of cultural particularism. Any society based on a rigorous application of human rights must, logically, claim to offer each ethnic group the scope to make its particular cultural contribution and to point to its achievements. However, this claim can only succeed if the framework created by these human rights is retained as the common point of reference.

Otherwise, all one is left with are ethnic groups (or groupings defined by other criteria such as religion or gender) confronting each other without any possibility of mediation or any superordinate system of standards for the regulation of conflict. This would mean that not just ethnic identity would be lost but all identity, and the survival of America as a coherent community would be seriously in question.

However, the idea of human rights as a normative frame of reference is undoubtedly of European origin. So the non-European "minorities" must resist the temptation to reject this frame of reference or to seek to relativize it. Conversely, the representatives of the "mainstream," the members of the European "majority" (in ethnic terms as well) have to be prepared not to resist further cultural "universalization."

At present, America is confronted in many areas of society with crises which, for the first time in its history, have thoroughly shaken the country's confidence that it can provide an example for the rest of the world to follow. Many people fear this marks the end of American claims to be a "chosen people." But it changes little with regard to America's real historical task – America is and remains the experimental laboratory for the creation of a genuinely universal society.

The impact of changing times
on American foreign policy

The recent changes on the domestic front in America have now started to cause significant shifts of emphasis in American foreign policy. Or, put another way, the disappearance of the external threat with the ending of the Cold War has given the USA breathing space during which it can turn its attention to domestic issues. It is only now that the sheer extent of the domestic problems, which have been building up over decades, has been fully realized.

Awareness of this significant turning point has already led to a crucial shift in priorities. More than ever before, American voters nowadays expect their politicians to concentrate almost exclusively on domestic affairs. Faced with the ambitious domestic policy agenda of the new, Republican-dominated Congress, any foreign contacts that congressmen are seen to cultivate are regarded as highly suspect by the electorate, because they distract attention from what are perceived as the real tasks at hand. This shift in priorities has, for example, already led to a situation whereby not one single American congressman traveled to Bonn or Berlin for political talks during the course of 1995.

However, the effects on the actual content of American foreign policy have been even more dramatic than this shifting of priorities. Since 1994 influential elements, in particular the Congress leadership, have devoted themselves to a far-reaching reinterpretation of American foreign policy, using the domestic challenges as a guideline for foreign policy initiatives as well. As in home affairs, they regard the USA as being unnecessarily constrained by excessive bureaucracy and inefficiency in terms of foreign policy, and generally take the view that US policy abroad has drifted too far from the ideas and interests of the American people.

In specific terms, the Chairman of the Senate Foreign Affairs Committee, Jesse Helms, and with him the Republican party, is demanding the abolition of numerous institutions, such as the United States Information Agency, which have for years been part of the foreign policy establishment in America. There are to be drastic cuts in development aid, and the size and number of US foreign missions are to be significantly reduced. Exchange programs for pupils and students, such as the Fulbright scholarships, which have been highly respected for decades, are to be dropped – apparently on the grounds that they are no longer important for American foreign policy or for the USA's image abroad.

Parallel to this, cooperation with international organizations is being subjected to critical scrutiny and attempts at radical reinterpretation. If it is the explicit aim of this domestic policy to recreate America's pioneer status in terms of its internal structures, then this "America first" policy, when translated into foreign affairs, means giving priority to national interests over multilateral obligations.

Last year, the main target of this policy was the United Nations. The UN was largely blamed for the fact that American foreign policy has suffered countless setbacks in recent years, ostensibly because the USA has been too closely bound by multilateral decision-making structures. Hence the failure of US involvement in Somalia under the UN flag, its ambivalent actions in Haiti, and its share in the failed UN policy in the former Yugoslavia.

One of the first things Congress has done since 1994 was restrict the scope for government cooperation with the UN. It was decided, for example, that no US troops would in future be deployed abroad under foreign (i.e. primarily UN) command. Furthermore, the funding to be made available to the UN for peacekeeping measures was to be cut further. Linked with this was a generally more restrictive approach to the deployment of American armed forces abroad. National interest is now given clear priority over global US security tasks in crisis regions of the world and this is a trend which has been accompanied by a general review of the stationing of troops overseas, including Europe.

This shift in foreign policy coordinates has sometimes been misinterpreted as a phenomenon which is due to a particular party, i.e. exclusively the new Republican majority. In fact, what is happening is a change of generation in both parties. In 1994 the number of deputies who were not reelected reached a climax unprecedented for twenty years. The younger, newly elected deputies, be they Democrats or Republicans, have almost unexclusively added attacks against the foreign policy concentration of the Washington establishment, which they considered unsuccessful, to their election campaigns. In the future this trend towards a change of generation will become even stronger. Almost all of those 13 senators who did not run for reelection in 1996 were committed to the transatlantic cause. Against the background of the present atmosphere in the American electorate, it seems highly unlikely that they will be substituted by like-minded politicians.

The proponents of this new American foreign policy strategy vehemently reject the suggestion, already made by the Europeans, that this is a prelude to a new period of American isolationism. The way they see it is that, on the contrary, they are concerned about reasserting America's claim to lead the world and to rid it of unnecessary ballast both in the form of unnecessary government bureaucracy and multilateral commitments. The proponents of this strategy can thus be best described as "unilateralists."

Their criticism that America has failed to assert its claim to world leadership in recent years may well be justified. However, it would be a mistake to conclude that the continued need for US involvement and leadership in the world can be served by a reduction of foreign policy resources.

The typical American domestic formulas for resisting "big government" cannot be regarded as a sort of panacea that can be applied to the field of foreign policy with the same results. It is precisely because the USA is having to concentrate increasingly on its own economic and social problems that renewed foreign policy efforts are required to ensure that the burden of the USA's international involvement, which is as necessary as ever, can be shared more efficiently with its allies and partners.

Despite this concentration on domestic affairs, the American public has always shown itself to be highly sensitive where foreign policy disasters are concerned, since these represent the most public contradiction of America's ongoing claim to role model status in the world. President Clinton, elected exclusively under the banner of domestic change, can ascribe his dramatic loss of popularity after his first couple of years in office largely to his neglect of foreign policy and the resulting disasters which occurred in various crisis regions of the world.

It is therefore unlikely that America will withdraw from world politics or even restrict itself to a more limited area of geopolitical interest. The Clinton administration has so far succeeded in defusing the most radical attempts at reorientation by opting for pragmatic compromises. Nevertheless, one should not underestimate the sheer extent of the present upheavals in the US domestic political scene. For the first time since the days of the New Deal in the thirties, whole sections of the population seem to be receptive to the idea of a radical change of paradigm in domestic policy: slimming down the state apparatus, which the Keynesian approach of President Roosevelt and his successors apparently allowed to run out of control, seems to be regarded by many Americans as the wonder drug that will revive the American Dream. Clinton was responding to this mood when he recently announced that the shedding of 200,000 public service jobs by his administration had brought the proportion of the working population employed in the public sector down to the same level as when Roosevelt took office in 1933.

If the success of this approach on the domestic front seems doubtful, then its transfer to the field of foreign policy, given the current conditions governing the USA's global responsibility, can only be characterized as bizarre, and therefore as a flight of fancy. Nevertheless, as recent events have demonstrated, one has to remain braced for repeated attacks on the US foreign policy "establishment" and its degree of global involvement. Politicians in the USA will have to consider carefully how they can justify to the public any continuation of the USA's involvement in international affairs, under new internal and external conditions. More importantly, they will have to consider what sacrifices they can demand in order to sustain such involvement. For the USA's European partners this means that even if America can still be relied upon to meet its international obligations, its role during this period of transition will be less easy to predict.

Europe in transition

Europe, too, is undergoing far-reaching changes in its self-perception and experiencing internal upheavals of an unpredictable nature. To a greater extent than in the USA, the reasons for this can be found in the radical structural changes resulting from the dawning of a new epoch in political terms. The transitional period which Europe finds itself in is characterized by the simultaneous coexistence of radical opposites. Processes of integration are occurring cheek-by-jowl with processes of disintegration – and both are affecting the European Union. Supranational political interweaving is running parallel to new splits along national lines. The old borders between Catholic and Orthodox Europe, between the Ottoman and Habsburg empires have reemerged. It is less clear than ever before where Europe begins and ends.

Unlike in the USA, it is not primarily economic or social problems that are creating unease and uncertainty about what the future holds in Europe. On the contrary, the prophets of doom in the 1980s, with their warnings that the European movement was grinding to a halt, have largely been silenced by Western Europe's dynamic economic development over the last ten years.

What is being questioned nowadays is whether, parallel to its economic success, Europe can also set up the necessary political structures – i.e. whether the process of European integration can be reconciled with the enlargement of the EU to take in ten to fifteen potential new members from Eastern Europe and the Mediterranean region.

This acceleration in the process of developing the EU is being met with a growing degree of skepticism at national level. The importance of national and regional concerns is increasing, and there are unmistakable signs of a partial return to classic patterns of thinking in terms of the balance of power within the EU. To gain a fundamental understanding of developments in Europe since 1989, all one has to do is to view them in these terms. It then immediately becomes clear why France is suddenly trying to push ahead with Monetary Union and why "Central European" Germany is once again being viewed in terms of what is claimed to be its national interests. It also explains why Germany is co-operating with Russia and is concerned about ensuring the survival of Ukraine.

At the same time this internationalization of economy and politics is intensifying, particularly where problems are concerned. But the development of appropriate decision-making structures at European level is still lagging behind and cannot yet offer an adequate response to pressures that are already too much for individual nation-states. Europe is trapped: on the one hand, the magnet of integration is attracting more and more politicians and states keen to accede to the EU. But on the other hand, the structures that would enable the Union to take political action at supranational level are not being developed quickly enough.

The continent is in danger of becoming a victim of its own success.

This simultaneity of contrasting developments is what makes Europe such a special case. The combination of hitherto unclear political constellations and new conflicts are making fresh demands on the Europeans, to which they still have to develop an adequate response. And it is from this complex Europe that America will demand a clear definition of its interests. It will expect Europe to have at its disposal the instruments with which it can pursue clearly defined interests. Thus, any realignment of the transatlantic partnership is going to require the Europeans to do some very basic homework.

As it struggles with its own identity crisis, Europe is not going to depart from the picture of America built up over the decades. The American contribution to the building of Europe and the joint victory in defending freedom against Communism has become a stable element in the European identity. As a result, Europe will thus continue to look to the USA and, despite the Americans' greater concentration on domestic affairs, they will continue to be regarded as Europe's primary and "natural" partners, both for the solution of internal European questions and also for provision of a joint response to global challenges.

New challenges

The end of the East-West conflict has resulted in obvious changes in the political map of Europe. Old allegiances have lost their importance and been replaced by new political force fields. And in the long term foreign policy orientations are set to change accordingly. The new alignments on the continent are beginning to emerge:

France has moved from the center of Western Europe to a position on the margins of the continent – all the more so as democracy and market economy gain a hold beyond Germany's eastern borders.

Prior to 1989, Europe did not have a center of any political relevance – and therefore avoided the problems of allegiance related to a central position. Since then, however, the old concepts have been revised: Germany now sees itself, albeit under different conditions, as part of the West but situated between East and West; Austria is faced with new, unprecedented claims, expectations and opportunities to exert influence on its flanks; and even Italy cannot turn a blind eye to the Balkan conflict – the Adriatic not only acts as a barrier, but is also a bridge. New zones are emerging within Europe:

- Southern Europe, the poorer member states of the European Community, whose material expectations are seen as competing with the East for resources;
- that part of Western Europe that contains the two nuclear powers from the old constellation, whose influence and political role are declining;
- the western part of Central Europe with Germany and Austria, which, despite their geographical position in the West, are most directly affected by developments in Eastern Europe;
- the Adriatic region with Italy, which is most strongly influenced by the upheavals in South Eastern Europe;
- the eastern part of Central Europe with Poland, Hungary, and the Czech and Slovak Republics, whose

ability to introduce reforms has widened the gap between them and their former partners within COMECON, but is not yet sufficient, in economic and political terms, to enable them to integrate into Western Europe;
– Northern Europe, which has lost its significance as a partially neutral area providing a gentle transition from West to East;
– Eastern Europe around the European part of Russia, whose future will be influenced by its political distance from and geographical proximity to Russia;
– Southeastern Europe, whose separation from West and East Central Europe has resulted from the ethnic conflicts and the political ambitions of the key states in the region, which have been partly latent and partly open.

All these regions lack homogeneous organizational structures. And it is still these locational differences that are responsible for differences in national and integrationist strategies. It is here that one has to look to find the reasons for the interest in deepening or widening the European Union; it is from here that the national concepts of integration, control and distribution of resources within the European Community are derived.

The new Europe is going through a stage of development that does not yet have a name attached to it. There is a lack of any clear pattern of events. What one finds instead is a development of dialectical tensions; in the West negotiations are under way for the deepening of a highly complex system of integration, but at the same time the region is experiencing signs of disintegration. Markets for goods and services throughout Europe are becoming increasingly internationalized, and yet at the same time the number of states, national markets and national currencies is on the increase. In Central Europe, military command systems are being peacefully dismantled, while at the same time the Balkans are experiencing appalling eruptions of primitive violence, destruction, alienation and hatred. As this region experiences conflicts from the inter-war period fought with weapons from the post-war era, one has to ask oneself what hope there is of providing a coherent form for a pan-European post-Communist order. Suddenly, the prevailing mood has become one of uncertainty.

The "return to Europe" is becoming a two-sided process: the peoples of Central and Eastern Europe are being confronted with an option for a future order which they do not yet seem to be ready for, and the peoples of Western Europe are being confronted with a part of their past that they thought they had long since come to terms with and left far behind.

The balance-of-power tactic

In a transitional era like the present one, the foreign policy of many states has reverted to what is a familiar pattern in the European context – that of maintaining a "balance of power." Behind the multilateralist rhetoric of the CSCE/OSCE, behind the wrangling about the heritage of the Soviet Union and the question of the timetable for accepting new members into the EU, there lie national calculations as to the best way to counterbalance the potential power wielded by neighboring states.

In Western Europe, European integration has become an instrument for such an approach. France has reacted to the shift in internal balance resulting from German unification by offering to deepen the European Union. Britain has countered the prospect of greater integration with the prospect of widening, in the expectation that this will lead to a looser type of integration. And the Southern Europeans have reacted to transfer payments from Western Europe to the transition states of the former Eastern bloc by coming up with new financial demands.

It is this return to the concept of a balance of power that holds the key to understanding both the conflict and the cooperation which we are at present witnessing both in Eastern and Western Europe. However, under present conditions, this process should not be seen as a return to the European tradition of grand diplomacy by nation states.

Politicians and societies may be harking back to centuries-old conflicts and strategies, but they cannot sidestep the conditions and instruments of economic interdependence and political interweaving. One of the peculiarities of the present-day policy of maintaining a balance of power is that it combines classic diplomacy with modern levels of integration. Even within the European Community, with its legal frameworks and political momentum, it is possible to pursue a policy of national interest; and the institutions of the Community and cooperative forms of decision-making are also suitable for achieving integration, control and balance.

As the continent develops its new order, this balance-of-power tactic will result in three developments:

- Firstly, one can expect a marked increase in conflict over questions of distribution amongst the states of Europe. One of the premises on which a balance-of-power policy is based is a degree of mistrust vis-à-vis the scope and ambitions of one's neighbors. Viewed in this light, integration becomes a zero sum game in which the aim is to retain one's present position.
- Secondly, this policy favors a tendency towards renationalization in an attempt to assure one's freedom to act. Faced with the prospect of deeper integration, the smaller states of Europe in particular fear a loss of their own rights of participation within the Community.
- Thirdly, this pattern tends to create structures which lack clear leadership, as any sign of one country assuming the role of leader immediately awakens a suspicion that it is bent on establishing a hegemony. This is the reason why there is broad support for the idea of the USA playing a role in Europe – so as to hinder the ambitions of potential leaders and defuse rivalries.

European politicians now face the task of giving some sort of form to these complex transitional constellations. National ambitions need to be brought into harmony with the challenges resulting from the situation. Europe cannot be constructed against the interests of the nations involved, but it is equally true that without European solutions, national interests cannot be protected.

This dialectic means that any attempt to play national interests off against European integration would have to be doomed to failure. Europe faces the challenge of transnational democracy: on the one hand there is growing pressure to organize the present level of mutual integration and shared sovereignty along democratic lines in future; and on the other hand the democratic order is itself becoming a European asset, the preservation of which can no longer be blocked on the grounds that it represents an impermissible "interference in the internal affairs" of a state.

Transition in Europe from an American perspective

From an American perspective, the many and seemingly diverse changes occurring in Europe must inevitably give rise to a degree of confusion and concern as to what form the future identity of their European partner is going to take. The attempts commonly undertaken to compare developments in Europe with the process by which America became a state and to base predictions on this will inevitably lead to misconceptions.

For the foreseeable future, Europe, even if it takes on the form of a close European Union, will remain a community of nation states, whereas the USA has never been a nation state in the traditional sense of the term. Irrespective of the history of the USA, creating Europe is not just a question of regulating the relationship between the individual and a state with the demands of the latter naturally increasing as society becomes more highly organized. In Europe the painful process of transferring centuries-old prerogatives from the individual states into the hands of the Union is also involved. And every time the Americans have demanded a common European response to urgent problems that could only be solved on a transatlantic basis, they have found out at their own expense that this process cannot be accelerated simply by exposure to the hard realities of world politics.

This different degree of organization amongst the transatlantic partners means that, from an American point of view, any realistic assessment of the scope for action available to the Europeans will have to keep in mind the prevailing asymmetry between the USA and Europe. The western community, the North Atlantic Alliance, still consists of one major world power and a series of small and medium-sized states on the other side of the Atlantic.

This discrepancy was not particularly relevant in the days when the East-West conflict still occupied the attention of the Alliance and when Western Europe was, furthermore, totally absorbed in its own reconstruction. But since then the inevitable question has become: when and how can Western Europe achieve unity and thus become a full-fledged partner?

From the very outset, the USA has given its sustained support to the western states' attempts at integration. It was prepared to accept the growth of a potential competitor because it expected Europe to be able to take some of the weight of global problems off American shoulders. This expectation has, however, not yet been fulfilled. European integration has turned out to be an economic success story, but in political terms Europe has not even come anywhere near being an equal partner for the USA. It has limped behind, above all because political union has not been able to keep up with economic integration.

Certainly, the Europeans succeeded in 1970 in creating the instrument of European Political Cooperation (EPC), which was to be replaced in 1993 by the Common Foreign and Security Policy (CFSP). Both of these have proved useful in establishing a general European position on certain issues. But in acute crises involving EU partners – most recently the war in Bosnia and

Croatia – the EPC and CFSP, because they are not binding, have regularly failed. They were of no use in coordinating the political strategy of the EU states in the former Yugoslavia.

Thus, the Europeans have to first of all find a response in terms of political union to the question of an appropriate form of organization for the western partnership. The more efficiently Europe succeeds in organizing itself, the easier it will be for the USA to enter into a long-term commitment in Europe. Europe has to use its economic strength to achieve a corresponding weight for itself in foreign and security policy, so as to strengthen the European pillar of the Alliance.

Up to now the USA has not been able to enter into a dialogue between equal partners – a prerequisite for keeping the Alliance alive in the longer term. When it asks what action the West should take, Washington regularly receives a range of different European responses.

The USA itself can contribute little to accelerating the process of clarification in Europe. It has learned in the past that Europe's internal dialogue is not susceptible to influence from the outside. Attempts to push through American objectives via close bilateral cooperation with individual EU member states have proved just as ineffective as occasional (more or less) gentle pressure exerted on the European Commission. A higher level partnership is only going to come about if the Europeans first become capable of such a partnership.

Strategies for the Europe of the future

It may well be the case that many Europeans consider any action based on maintaining equilibrium as, for the time being, an adequate solution. However, this is not an appropriate way of solving far-reaching challenges and, in particular, does not do justice to America's expectations regarding a more mature partnership.

Rather, the current political problems demand that European politicians come up with strategic responses in four areas in particular, namely changes to the institutions responsible for integration – including their capacity to act, the further development of the EU towards a true political, Economic and Monetary Union, stabilizing and integrating Central and Eastern Europe; and finally, preserving peace and security on the continent.

The Maastricht Treaty

The Maastricht Treaty, which came into force on November 1, 1993, was Europe's first attempt at a comprehensive response to the challenges set by the new era. The European Union, which this Treaty officially created, is based on three pillars: the European Community (EC), the Common Foreign and Security Policy (CFSP) and cooperation in the fields of Justice and Home Affairs (JHA).

The most radical changes are likely to come from monetary union which, as part of the first pillar (EC), is scheduled for the end of the decade. In practice, this means that the citizens of Europe will see their national currencies abolished in favor of a single currency for the whole of Europe.

With respect to Common Foreign and Security Policy, a series of steps – but no fixed timetable – has been established according to which the CFSP will not only entail the development of a common security policy but will be followed by a common defense policy, which may in turn, lead to common defense.

As for Justice and Home Affairs, the third pillar of the European Union as provided for in the Maastricht Treaty, future developments remain hazy. Preparations have, however, already given rise to a flurry of ideas concerning integration aimed at developing joint mechanisms for the years to come – ranging from policies on asylum, refugees and immigration to internal security, organized crime and the smuggling of nuclear material.

In the Treaty this catalog of measures is complemented by partial reform of the decision-making processes in the EU's institutions. For example, the principle of qualified majority voting is to be extended into a number of additional areas, thus reinforcing the position of the Community's institutions vis-à-vis the member states.

In sum, the Maastricht Treaty also points the way towards a qualified deepening of the European Union. The new instability prevailing in Europe following the collapse of the Communist bloc has set Maastricht against the objective of the forced – indeed irreversible when it comes to monetary policy – integration of EU member states. Deeper integration would be an effective barrier against the centrifugal tendencies of the new era and could lead to a complete revival of traditional balance-of-power politics in Europe. Deepening the Union is also crucial if the door is going to be opened to new member states from Eastern Europe, since a

European Union of 20 or even 25 states would, if the existing cumbersome decision-making structures are not reformed, lead to complete paralysis of the Community's institutions.

There is still cause to doubt whether the Maastricht Treaty can fulfill the ambitious demands for further development of the Union. A look back at the debate over ratification already raises the question whether the noble wording of the Treaty is really matched by a true desire for integration on the part of its signatories. Ratification of the Treaty was just barely attained referenda in Denmark, Ireland and France and was accompanied by debate on its compatibility with existing constitutional arrangements in the UK and in Germany. In many EU member states, the debate on the Treaty's ratification led to polarization in matters of policy on Europe the like of which had never previously been experienced. For the first time, policy on European integration became a controversial issue at the heart of the domestic political agenda.

The intensity of the debate is surprising, too, since the Treaty on European Union only lays down in permanent form those areas where there is basic consensus on the part of the member states. Political Union, which is especially desired by Germany, is not included in the wording of the Treaty, nor are effective mechanisms to deal with the coordination of financial policy once member states have signed up for Monetary Union. Pushing through the desired deepening of the Union despite the Maastricht Treaty's obvious shortcomings concerning integration and the growing degree of skepticism being displayed by Europe's citizens will prove to be the central challenge facing European politics in the next five years. As has been seen from the newly fanned flames of the debate on Monetary Union that is currently raging within Germany, European integration is set to tie up a great deal of political energy in the immediate future and will progressively mean that Europe – perhaps to an even greater degree than the USA – is going to have to turn its attention inwards in order to safeguard the objectives anchored in the Maastricht Treaty.

The difficulties involved in implementing the plans to deepen the Union are unmistakable. For example, the stability objectives ("convergence criteria..."), which are prerequisites for the introduction of a single currency, require the member states to display economic discipline, particularly with regard to their budgets. Yet, owing to the unexpected recession of 1992–93, as well as other factors, this goes way beyond the capabilities of many countries. At present, only a few states come anywhere near meeting the criteria for the third stage of Monetary Union and some member states are so far from fulfilling the convergence criteria that it looks unlikely that they will ever be able to join if the Treaty's provisions regarding monetary union are adhered to strictly.

A Common Foreign and Security Policy also appears to be on shaky ground. Faced with the resurgence of national approaches, NATO reform and the revival of the WEU, the Europeans are tentatively edging towards new structures in a way that leaves a great deal hanging in the balance. When it comes to institutional reform – i.e. introducing a more streamlined decision-making process within the Council and/or between the Council and the Commission – it also appears doubtful, given the bitter debate on qualified majority voting that arose in 1994, whether the objectives decided upon at Maastricht will ever be given a chance to succeed.

These examples together with the question of internal security within the Union – i.e. the third pillar of the Treaty – demonstrate the heart of the debate on deepening the Union. Not all the existing fifteen member states are in a position to meet these objectives, neither do all of them desire to do so. Traditional national reservations and sensibilities, which would have to be overcome at every stage of deepening and/or enlargement, are crucial in this respect.

Furthermore, there is an essential, more serious, problem: many EU citizens feel that the Union lacks transparency. They think that, these days, the complicated mechanisms of European policy-making and administrative structures function primarily to serve the interests of European bureaucracy rather than the need to regulate everyday life within the EU.

The process of European unification began from above, with broad-based support from the citizens of the original member states. As integration progressed, governments became increasingly negligent in consolidating the European institutions' legitimacy in the eyes of the citizens. The latest pinnacle in this development is the Maastricht Treaty. Both in terms of the quantity and quality of the provisions it contains, it goes way beyond all previous agreements within the EU. A great deal of its provisions are so complex that, in many cases, even the signatories only grasped their true significance afterwards.

This was the reason why the public debate on the Treaty's ratification tended to focus less on objective discussion of the Treaty's contents. Rather, the almost mythical lack of transparency in the Treaty on European Union meant that it had a nigh on magnetic ability to attract the confused worries, fears and reservations of the citizens of Europe.

The apparent apathy with regard to gaining public acceptance is particularly striking since it ties in with an increasing tendency to become disillusioned with politics, which is apparent throughout Western Europe. Thanks to a series of revelations focusing on abuse of power and corruption in the corridors of political and economic power, many citizens are gaining the impression that society's decision-makers merely serve the complicated system they themselves have created, and that they have lost sight of the true interests of the people they ought to be representing.

At another level the EU is having to tackle the same phenomenon that is basically responsible for the sea change in domestic policy in the USA. Many Americans believe that the traditional practices of political decision-making have developed into an impenetrable labyrinth, and they have serious doubts about its legitimacy and efficiency. For the average American, Washington has become a synonym for overorganized and useless bureaucracy, similar to the image that Brussels has had among critics of European integration for some time now. Hence, it is imperative that both America and Europe make fundamental changes to their politics and administration based on the twin benchmarks of acceptance and efficiency. If they do not succeed, there is a risk that both transatlantic partners will be rendered impotent on both the domestic and international fronts as a result of their citizens' growing reluctance to accept unfathomable strategies aimed at solving both national and international problems.

The European Union has called an Intergovernmental Conference (IGC) for 1996/1997 that will determine the way forward; it is intended to give the process of integration new impetus and pave the way for amendments to the Maastricht Treaty. The whole idea of taking integration further will thus be subjected to careful consideration.

Unlike previous EU reforms, the run-up to "Europe '96" has become the topic of much heated debate in the domestic political arena of many member states. While the debate on the imminent reforms is gaining momentum, the quality of debate is suffering. Too many voices are speaking at once; the whole debate is too confused and the contributions are too tactically calculated and confusing for any clear line to emerge. Alongside the attempts to lower expectations as regards reform, there are dramatic calls for a comprehensive reconfiguration of Europe's institutions and mechanisms. Furthermore, policy on Europe is considered to lack legitimacy and acceptance. An open debate on the future of Europe is being called for – and rightly so.

The development of European unification can be described as a history of attempts at reform. Successful changes rub shoulders with missed opportunities. If one looks closely, Europe '96 is an abbreviation for the twelfth round of the fundamental debate on adjusting European structures so as to bring them into line with the current situation on the continent. And this is indicative of the first dilemma. Discussion on Europe '96 is developing as though the old line of development merely requires a few articles to be added to it, thus carrying on where Maastricht left off, hence adding to

a Treaty that is already unprecedented in its complexity
and lack of transparency.

The preparations for Europe '96 are copying this pattern nigh on perfectly: labyrinthine channels of discussion, an absence of public debate and a technocratic
obsession with detail. In the process we seem to be for-
getting that Maastricht only avoided failure by a hair's
breadth. Every well-informed observer has to realize
that Maastricht was the last time the Europeans would
accept such a state of affairs. However, we are continuing to prepare Maastricht II as though nothing had
happened. One does not require much imagination to
predict that the plans are condemned to failure because, in the end, the citizens of Europe will refuse to
play along.

The approaches to reform

None of the classic terms defined by political science
can describe the current level of integration appropriately: neither a federal state, nor a confederacy of su-
preme governments nor a union of fatherlands. The
status quo is nothing more than the gradual extension
of the forming of a functional community, a process
which began back in the 1950s with six founding members; it may be more complex but the old logic remains.
Both in the days of the Europe of Twelve, and now with
the Fifteen, this logic comes at a high price: drastic re-
ductions in Europe's capacity to take action. Europe
'96, however, has to serve as the blueprint for a twenty-
member Europe and, in the medium term, for a Europe
that encompasses thirty member states.

The EU's current fields of competence are the result of a certain rank growth. Integration has reached a saturation point that forces every new step to be justified anew. It is nonsensical to welcome blindly every new step towards further integration. The dream of the post-war era has, to a great extent, come true – simply to repeat it would be inappropriate because we now live in different times. Rather, the Union is going to have to find ways out of the success trap, this being a suitable expression because the Union's attractiveness means it is having to take on more and more tasks without having the mechanisms and structures to keep pace.

Since Maastricht, Europe has found itself in difficulties. This means the asymmetry of monetary union on the one hand and Political Union on the other. While Monetary Union is precisely defined with fixed criteria and instruments, political union is restricted to a limited set of approaches. It is, of course, clear that Monetary Union cannot function without being accompanied by appropriate economic, countercyclical and financial policies. Therefore, putting an end to the difficulties posed by Maastricht remains an urgent task for the EU.

Establishing the powers and instruments of the EU

The European Union, while taking into account the new circumstances of international politics, needs to discover its essential meaning. Simply adding one extra treaty to the fifteen that are valid today within the Union is impossible, if only because of the very sensitive issue of public acceptance. The Union must be oriented towards the essential. Every political system – including the European Union – has to achieve certain basic results: it must guarantee the liberty and freedom of movement of its citizens, reliably maintain a common legal system, create the conditions for economic prosperity and guarantee security both within and outside its borders.

Any reform has to measure up to these categories and the Union's areas of competence have to be ordered according to these criteria. These days even experts have to engage in comprehensive and time-consuming research if they want a precise overview of the separation of powers. No political system can survive long-term if it is based on such impenetrable foundations. We urgently need an overview of EU jurisdiction that provides a clear explanation of who is responsible for what in such a manner that it can be understood by everyone.

Transparency thanks to a bicameral system

The objectives of effectiveness and transparency must, at the same time, be combined with the principle of democracy. All three therefore interact with one another. The solution would inevitably be to simplify procedures, reducing them to a form that is common in all traditional democracies in Europe. This would suggest a bicameral system as the basic model for European policy-making:

- The Council of Ministers of the European Union would be one chamber, representing the crucial role of the member states.
- The European Parliament would, as the second chamber, represent the direct source of authority in

Europe for those decisions not falling under any other jurisdiction.
– The logic of this proposal means that the Commission, as the executive, would be nominated by the European Parliament and approved by the European Council.

Defining European foreign and security policy

The European Union has to guarantee security both within and outside its borders. This is one of the European Community's raisons d'être. The development of the Common Foreign and Security Policy (FSP) needs to progress in such a manner that it guarantees the European Union's ability to take action – rather than the succession of caricatures for which the European Union supplies material on a daily basis. Existing arrangements with regard to European security have to be brought into line with the new reality in Europe. This includes setting up a collective security system that gives equal weighting to American and European interests.

Differentiated integration

Given the inestimable magnetism of the Union, the key topic of "being able to act" is set to become even more crucial in almost every field of activity; from a Europe of Six to today's Europe of Fifteen, then on to a Europe of 21, 25, even 28 states in years to come, with around 500 million citizens. This begs the decisive question as to how such a community of states, boasting such tremendous heterogeneity, can possibly be organized, be it politically, economically or culturally.

Anyone making a careful study of the history of European unification is bound to come across differentiation as the key to success. From the very beginning there have been different forms of organization, varying paces for putting measures into practice. The larger and more heterogeneous the territory to be integrated is, the greater the necessity for differentiation will become. In the future, political union, Common Foreign and Security Policy, Economic and Monetary Union and the single market will not all involve the same member states. Such a complicated system can only remain organized, however, if it follows a calculated course – rather than being prey to ill-thought-out random action. The European Union therefore needs a plan that can organize integration at a high level but also at varying speeds.

The search for a European identity

Beyond spur-of-the-moment tactics and the imponderables of reform, the reasons for the present insecurity in Europe go far deeper. At the moment Europe has no response to the essential strategic questions of the new political age. There must be more behind this failing than a current loss of political form. Without a doubt the politico-cultural substance of such a European state has been affected by turmoil in the world political scene. Crises in domestic politics and question marks with regard to power politics are inevitable. But these more superficial findings disguise the real problem. Europe lacks the notion of a European order.

Every era in European history is interfaced with cultural patterns and drafts aimed at shaping the continent. From the Greek notion of democracy, via the Roman Empire and the tension between Church and State in the Middle Ages, to the era of nation-states and the conflict between Communism and democracy this century – every era had the notion of an order that structured the thinking and actions of the Europeans, an order that formed the essence of the European identity.

However, the structure that this idea provided disappeared with the collapse of Communism and the end of the division of the continent. Europe has to find a new order and use it to establish her identity anew.

America and the Europe of the future

At first glance it appears paradoxical: of all the times to start raising the issue of the continent's leading role, the Americans have to do so in a period of deep-seated insecurity about the future shape of Europe. Given its increasing problems at home, America, which has ended up as the only global power after the collapse of the Soviet Union, is applying more and more pressure on the Europeans to play a greater role in solving global problems.

While it is true that disagreement on the appropriate way to share military, political and financial burdens has always permeated the history of the western alliance, the end of the East-West conflict has given this dispute a completely new quality for two reasons.

Firstly, America's absolute military dominance has been transformed into mere relative superiority following the decline of nuclear deterrence, which has sunk into insignificance. Many of the Alliance's military operations today – such as in Bosnia – could, from a purely technical point of view, just as easily be carried out by European forces alone.

Secondly, owing to the disappearance of an external threat, the American public has begun to exert far stronger pressure than before on its government to channel all available resources into solving the gigantic domestic challenges it faces. The US Administration is finding it more and more difficult to get the go-ahead for international financial commitments, or even to get Congress and the people to agree to American soldiers participating in international peace missions. Regardless of worries within Europe about Maastricht I and II, American pressure on the Europeans to step up their contribution to all financial, military and political stability missions worldwide is therefore set to increase.

It is thus in the Americans' interests that Europe learns, as soon as possible, to speak with one voice politically, militarily and economically or at least to channel the chorus of voices more effectively. Those admonitory American voices wishing to prevent a stronger Europe (with regard to defense policy) becoming more independent and perhaps ending its alliance with the USA are unlikely to subside. However, because of the increased urgency of the problem, which urges a greater sharing of the burden, those American politicians who openly advocate European integration are, for the foreseeable future, going to keep the upper hand.

This also applies to economic relations for here, too, America is set to benefit if, thanks to progress in European integration, the slowest ship in the European convoy will no longer be able to block forward-looking strategies for economic partnership with the USA.

And it is not only the deepening of the EU that is in America's interest. The same goes for enlargement. Allowing new member states from Eastern Europe to join the European Union will contribute enormously to their internal stability and thus reduce the probability of crisis and conflict in this region considerably. This is of particular interest to the United States because – as the Bosnian conflict confirmed – a crisis in Europe always requires direct action by the United States before it can be resolved.

Moreover, allowing Eastern European states to join the EU would reduce the pressure for NATO enlargement because EU accession would already make these countries part of a western area of stability, thus reducing their need for an additional guarantee of security. This, in turn, would be in the particular interests of the Americans, both in terms of domestic and foreign policy. At home, it is extremely doubtful whether, given the current situation, the majority needed to extend American NATO commitments to Eastern Europe could be achieved, and on the foreign policy front NATO enlargement remains one of the main differences separating the United States and Russia.

There are still fears within the United States that the European Union will use the integration of Eastern Europe to turn this area into a kind of European "chasse gardée," at least in economic terms. Such considerations are, however, set to remain secondary to the benefits America would gain from these countries joining the EU. In the future, America will take every available opportunity to urge the EU to speed up the process of accession for the states of Eastern Europe.

Paradoxically, precisely because it has to devote more attention to domestic political problems, America has to seek much closer solidarity with the Europeans when it comes to solving international problems. America, as Europe's main partner, takes on the important role of constantly reminding the Europeans not to get tied up in seemingly trivial internal quarrels relating to European integration and not to lose sight of wider global challenges.

Whether it is aware of the fact or not, Europe has to bear responsibility worldwide simply because of her economic might and, together with the United States, has already become one of the main sources of hope in the world when it comes to support for democracy and economic liberalization. In future, the USA will increasingly remind the Europeans of their duty to take on the political responsibility commensurate with their position as a world economic power.

As for the Europeans, they will be continually reminded of America's significance as their main partner. And this will also apply during the imminent processes of widening and deepening the European Union. At the outset, however, Europe's familiar "equilibrium reflex" will be important. Whenever a European nation fears a sustained shift in the economic and political balance of the continent that may not work in its favor it tries to bring the USA into play as a guarantor of equilibrium. This reflex has been visible once again in the preparations for Maastricht II. For example, the Transatlantic Free Trade Area (TAFTA) proposed by the Germans has been hijacked by Euroskeptics in some member states in an attempt to portray transatlantic free trade as an alternative to forced integration within the European Union.

The current world political situation means, however, that using the United States as a referee and guarantor of equilibrium within Europe is no longer in tune with the times. Furthermore, America is not going to be prepared to play along in the future. In the last fifty years, Western Europe has achieved a level of political and economic stability that ought to render unnecessary additional one-sided efforts on the part of the Americans in order to guarantee peace within Europe and to ensure equilibrium between European partners. America no longer wishes to play the saint of the new European order as was the case during the post-war era but, rather, is far more interested in a symmetrical partnership that includes Europe as an equal in international politics with all the rights – and especially the new obligations – this entails.

Today, Europe has the full potential to take on this new role of an equal partner with the United States. One condition for the full exploitation of this potential is that the Europeans are politically aware of the new international challenges that have emerged in the wake of the end of the Cold War. If they fail to react to these challenges, or if they react inadequately, the risk of permanent erosion of the Transatlantic Community exists, since in its quest for partners who are prepared to share the burden the USA will increasingly begin casting its nets outside Europe.

Thus, with regard to relations with the United States, too, the reform of the European Union that is now on the agenda must not be allowed to become a mere extension of previous steps towards reform. None of the developments within the European Community and/or Union in recent decades has had any effect on the fundamental asymmetry in relations between Europe and

America. Europe has gained economic strength and is becoming an ever keener rival to the United States, but politically America's dominance in determining and conducting western strategies even remained unaffected when the Americans opted to delegate responsibility to the Europeans.

A true reform of the European Union must help to overcome this asymmetry in the relationship. This means that the transatlantic angle has to be an integral part of the debate on Maastricht II for this is the only way that the European partners will recognize the global nature of reforms that many in Europe regard as a purely European affair. Including the Americans does not – as many will misinterpret it – mean allowing the Americans to make decisions in Brussels, to sit in on the cabinet discussions of the European government, so to speak. Rather, coordinating reform with the United States means working out in advance the consequences for Europe's main partner of the objectives of European integration – such as the development of a Common Foreign and Security Policy. It also means including in the equation cooperation with the USA as an equal partner. This is the only way for the European Union to introduce reforms that take into account the situation outside Europe's borders and that contribute to creating a new order for Europe with a modern, internationalist outlook.

Towards a new transatlantic community

Between drift and new order – is the transatlantic cultural split inevitable?

What are the consequences of internal social and political changes on both sides of the Atlantic for the transatlantic relationship? We are dealing with two parties that both find themselves in a – more or less serious – identity crisis. On the verge of their entry into a new era, the members of the transatlantic partnership lack a firm sense of direction. It is becoming increasingly difficult for Europe and America to calculate one another's actions – especially as the weighting of economy, security and culture shifts. Under circumstances such as these, conflicts could be triggered off very easily.

But in times of international insecurity, these weaknesses may also strengthen transatlantic relations. Neither partner is capable of solving their problems alone; neither partner is likely to find effective assistance elsewhere. As a result, both will attempt to seek stability by shoring up the other. On the other hand, neither partner is yet in a position to describe clearly their international role in the changed international arena, nor have they succeeded in defining their interests in a convincing manner.

The terms of reference of transatlantic cooperation have changed immensely as a result of the end of the Cold War. Even if the familiar, tried and tested structures of cooperation are still in place, the coordinates of cooperation between the two partners and the focus of their actions are certainly changing, perhaps imperceptibly at first but, at times, with striking clarity.

As far as the transatlantic partners are concerned, the disappearance of the threat posed by the Warsaw Pact has also meant the disappearance of the core motivation for joint action with a specific objective. The joint defense mission as a guiding principle and protective shield, under which all differences in all areas could be subsumed, now constitutes an ever declining part of the new agenda.

Crises beyond NATO's domain, trade conflicts both within and outside the western community, global challenges such as environmental pollution or nuclear terrorism have moved to the fore as topics demanding a high level of political decision, yet the transatlantic partners have no commonly accepted guidelines for dealing with them. Differences on individual issues which have always existed are now becoming clearly visible and are being allowed to develop unchecked.

Against this background any European or American initiatives limited to a regional approach have become much more sensitive issues than before. European observers have taken to pointing to Asia-Pacific Economic Cooperation (APEC), the free trade project between the USA and its Pacific neighbors, or the Free Trade Association of the Americas (FTAA) in the pan-American region as evidence of America beginning to turn its back on the old continent. Likewise, many experts in the USA suspect that deepening the European Union and enlarging it towards the east augurs the reappearance, this time in a more spectacular form, of the specter of a fortress Europe.

None of these developments can, however, disguise the fact that, in the foreseeable future, there is no alternative to the transatlantic relations that have grown up over the last fifty years. During this period Europe and America have created a network of relations which is unprecedented throughout the world. The western partners have succeeded in building up more common understanding as regards democracy, pluralism, human rights and market economy than has ever been the case in history to date; and what is more, this common understanding is being accepted by, and serving as a model for, more and more nations all over the world.

Why is this uninterrupted success story being pushed further and further onto the sidelines of public awareness? There is a lack of common orientation, no new agenda to take into account the altered external conditions and to tap into the inexhaustible spring of joint energies.

In order to establish transatlantic consensus the old structures left over from the era of conflict between East and West are still being used. But these structures do not go far enough to meet new challenges. Changing the old backdrops and, as a result, using common consensus to tackle precisely the tasks of the future requires new guiding principles for common action. It is becoming increasingly obvious that the capability for developing this new outline for a common direction in transatlantic relations will ultimately decide their fate.

If one does not react decidedly to this challenge, a transatlantic cultural split in Euro-American relations seems inevitable, whose effects would radically call the structure of those links formed during the past fifty years into question. This split in the culture of political and social contact with each other would not come about in the form of abrupt cuts or spectacular arguments; it would, by contrast, lead in the medium term to a perpetual drifting apart of attitudes and subjective designs of the decision-makers in politics and social life on both sides of the Atlantic.

Signs of a possible start of this process have already today become manifest in the creeping erosion of bilateral links. Thus the parliamentarian contacts between Europe and the USA have recently been visibly thinning. According to American insiders, in the policyplanning of the American executive, the transatlantic relationship is also moving to the fringe of the operative radar screen. If this trend continues and extends over other fields, in the medium term the know-how and the tried and tested routine of transatlantic coordination will disappear. In consequence, the previously broad flow of information would peter out and Euro-American attention would cool.

At present these tendencies are still hidden by various surfacing symptoms of the extremely facetious transatlantic points of contact. Euro-American tourism, which has doubled during the past two decades, the multiplication of mailing and telecommunications as well as the growing mutual penetration of markets with products from transatlantic partners are all said to be signs of the increasingly deeper and indissoluble cultural connection between Europe and America. The concentration on these manifestations neglects that in recent years the mobility of products, services and news has exponentially increased globally, i. e. not only in the Euro-American sector. However, this development has been unable to prevent that many of the regions and states which have become more closely connected by this new mobility are still dealing most severely and partly with warlike means with their conflicts.

Real cultural solidarity must be borne by a more deeply grounded willingness to negotiate and an interest in the partner's society. In the last fifty years, these dispositions were successfully established and widely fixed on all levels of society by the permanent commitment of convinced advocates of the transatlantic partnership. If this commitment diminished due to focusing on other social issues the potential of transatlantic cultural solidarity which has already evolved would inevitably be endangered.

As this erosion is below the surface, the whole extent of the presently existing split would become visible only when the damage could no longer be repaired according to the reliable pattern of direct contacts via pulling the relevant strings. The precondition for this is the permanent cultivation of the culture of political and social contacts as well as a high level of agreement concerning the expectations towards each other. As soon as the attitudes of leading opinion makers in Europe and America have drifted apart, thus leading to far-reaching diverging results, the basis for short-term successful crisis management will also vanish

The consequence of such a shift of coordinates would be that necessarily inconsistent individual decisions would be reverted to, as continuous Euro-American structural dispositions – e.g. the common security policy – increasingly become indistinct. Moreover, the partners would pursue their policy towards others on their own, as a common concept of mutual consultation would equally get lost as would the common political contents. Thus, Europeans and Americans would inevitably turn towards those regions which demand the immediate attention of daily politics, i.e. Europe towards the east of the continent and the Mediterranean region, the USA towards its own hemisphere as well as the Pacific Rim.

This process would not only lead to a far-reaching drifting apart of political and social orientations, but also – in the worst case – to a direct political split between Europe and America, i.e. to a complete abandonment of the concept of the fundamental community of interests. The danger of such a cultural split can be surmounted only if a future-oriented concept for deepening the transatlantic relationship can be developed which takes both partners' topical interests into consideration. Without this strategic-perspective renewal of the Euro-American community, its existence and success is in question. Recently James Thomson, President of the RAND Corporation, which is presumably the most important American thinktank, urgently warned Europeans and Americans: "If the Euro-American relationship is not fundamentally deepened and enlarged, it will die." Without deepening the Transatlantic Community between Europe and America in a way that is both in tune with the times yet also geared towards the future, the existence and success of the Transatlantic Community is in question.

The search for a new direction

In order to develop a new direction for common action the transatlantic partners require a binding basis. Back in 1990, immediately after the 'abdication' of its former adversary in the East, the western alliance was already feeling the need for new impetus regarding cohesion within its ranks. On November 23, 1990, immediately after the CSCE conference in Paris sanctioning the new order in Europe, the European Community and the USA adopted the "Transatlantic Declaration" outlining the future of relations between Europe and America.

This declaration was an impressive affirmation of the successes achieved since the war, particularly with respect to democracy, human rights and the free market economy. The partners committed themselves to furthering these principles throughout the world and established a series of consultative mechanisms aimed at reinforcing transatlantic cooperation at all significant policy levels as well as cooperation on social issues.

Bolstered with optimism as a result of the success in overcoming Communism in Europe, there were high expectations that a resolute demonstration of Transatlantic Community spirit was all that was required to advance the western success stories of democracy, human rights, the peaceful settlement of conflict and free market economy all over the world. The "New World Order" proclaimed by the then US President, George Bush, was a precise expression of this vision. It called on the states of the western world, in particular, to regard themselves, in the wake of the East-West conflict, as a community of global problem-solvers, charged with ridding the world of military conflict, human rights violations and economic misery once and for all. Hence, the end of the East-West conflict was seen as a turning point which, once passed, meant that all the global evil that had supposedly been caused by this conflict could now be eradicated thanks to resolute cooperation.

The rapid victory in the Gulf conflict over the aggression of Saddam Hussein notched up in February 1991 by the coalition of American and Western allied forces initially seemed to provide fresh sustenance to the new optimism of the architects of the New World Order. Very rapidly, however, it became obvious that even after the disappearance of the nuclear threat posed by the Warsaw Pact, the world was still a very dangerous place. The limits of western problem-solving strategies were clearly brought home in Somalia and Haiti between 1992 and 1994. And ultimately the four-year drama in the former Yugoslavia has been more than a clear demonstration of the western community's inability to prevent brutal human rights violations and aggression on its own doorstep; it has also shown the real danger of the disintegration of the West as a result of the centrifugal forces of a crisis for which there were no agreed patterns of response nor structures aimed at bringing it to an end, such as had existed during the Cold War for the eventuality of possible aggression by the Warsaw Pact, for example.

As a result, compared with the year of change between 1989 and 1990 the outlook for the future was far more sobering. The global challenges of war, ethnically motivated atrocities, famine, terrorism etc. proved too stubborn to enable the West to solve them merely with a swift, concerted show of strength. In any case, the growing domestic challenges facing America and Europe appear to make such a show of strength increasingly difficult to accomplish. It is therefore only logical, and in line with political realism, that the concept of a "New World Order" quietly slipped out of political usage. However, this farewell also heralded the disappearance of the western community's last common vision, that of setting a forward-looking course oriented towards tackling new global tasks.

Together with the disappearance of a common vision and orientation, there have recently been increased signs that the traditional close-knit cooperation between America and Europe has begun to unravel slightly. In the last three years 200,000 American soldiers have left Europe, most of whom (150,000) were stationed in Germany. Their departure also means bidding farewell to many German-American cultural associations, exchange programs and social events.

In other areas of inter-cultural exchange, too, cuts are being made and institutes closed, especially by the Americans – witness the closing in 1995 of the 'America Houses' in Hanover and Stuttgart. In general, we are witnessing the scaling down of the Americans' special political and social interest in Europe over the last fifty years as a front line against Communism, against which they felt obliged to defend Western Europe. Inevitably this is reflected in the intensity of political contacts, too. In 1995, for example, not one single American Congressman paid a visit to Bonn because – unlike in the past – contact with German politicians can no longer be portrayed to the average American voter as an act of defense by the whole of the free West against an external threat.

Recently, the unraveling of the net of transatlantic relations, the lack of a common new direction and the ensuing dangers of substantial erosion, in the medium term, of the Euro-American partnership have been felt more and more painfully by many players on both sides of the Atlantic. All parties involved realized that the "Transatlantic Declaration" adopted in 1990, with its ultimately non-binding structures for cooperation, was inadequate for the true reestablishment of a Transatlantic Community.

Thus, new models for the future prospects of Euro-American cohesion are being drawn up with increasing intensity. Leading European and American politicians, in particular the German Minister for Foreign Affairs, Klaus Kinkel, and his American counterpart, Warren Christopher, have declared their support for new treaty arrangements between Europe and the USA, as well as for the drawing-up of a binding transatlantic agenda or the establishment of new forums for cooperation at all conceivable levels.

Some of these ideas proceed on a pragmatic and inductive basis. They begin at those points where common ground initially appears possible, such as the mutual protection of foreign investments or the harmonization of product standards and norms. The hope is that, by instituting new forms of Euro-American cooperation that begin at the bottom and work upwards, it will be possible to create, for example, a common economic area.

Other proposals take existing structures of cooperation and build on them. For example, the enlargement of NATO to include the new democracies of Central and Eastern Europe is regarded as an opportunity to give relations between Europe and America a forward-looking perspective in line with the modern era. Moreover, renowned politicians on both sides of the Atlantic have called for this new beginning to be given concrete shape in the form of a "Transatlantic Treaty" or a "Transatlantic Charter."

All these approaches have one thing in common, namely the worry about the creeping erosion of the transatlantic partnership following the disappearance of the common foe. Any reshaping of cooperation to bring it in line with the times – a move which is absolutely imperative – cannot simply be derived from everyday political practice but has to be given a structure that is binding for all partners involved. Yet so far, approaches have tended to get bogged down in too much detail as a result of the present lack of a clear and all-encompassing leading interest, as provided by security policy during the Cold War. None of the individual areas of present-day and future cooperation mentioned above can, if taken alone, offer a newly founded Transatlantic Community a solid foundation.

Together with the rush of new ideas and proposals, there has also been a host of critics voicing their misgivings. Unlike the advocates' all-encompassing visions for politics as a whole, the critics focus their efforts on individual elements of the models proposed, bemoaning their lack of feasibility.

Here we have to distinguish between two groups of critical arguments. On the one hand, there is doubt as to whether the implementation of certain individual proposals is in the interests of the transatlantic partners. Objections to an enlargement of NATO, for example, focus on worries that this may lead to a new demarcation line in Europe. The critics of a transatlantic free trade area point out that around 90 percent of trade in goods between Europe and America is not subject to tariffs anyway and that it would be preferable to concentrate on other, more specialized areas such as harmonizing product standards and norms for example. This group of arguments may, despite all the criticism of the new initiatives contained therein, be extremely helpful when it comes to clarifying the substance of any future transatlantic common ground.

For the supporters of a revival in transatlantic relations, there is, however, a second category of objections that are much more worrying since they are based on the assumption that the interests of Europe and America are far too diverse to allow the existence of any cooperation structures more binding than those already in place. As a result, any attempt at closer cooperation would result in transatlantic incompatibilities becoming even more pronounced and could even contribute to the breakdown of existing relations. By way of example, it was only during negotiations on a transatlantic free trade area that the differences between Europe and America with respect to policy on the trade of agricultural goods, textiles and steel were first brought home to many people. The idea of a broadly-based transatlantic free trade agreement between the European Union and the USA could, if it failed to find safe passage through Congress, definitively sour relations between the two partners. By the same token, any reflection on NATO enlargement could result in the whole issue of America's security guarantee for Europe being called into question.

As evidence of these hypotheses and as an argument against a more permanent form of political consultation, reference is made to actual or perceived differences in opinion between Europeans and Americans when it comes to the numerous crisis regions of the world and/or international challenges. Whether with respect to Bosnia, the question of allowing Russia to join NATO, policy towards Iran's or North Korea's nuclear capability, tackling terrorism in the Middle East or dealing with trade conflicts with Japan, fundamental differences between European and American attitudes have emerged that are all calling into question the advisability of closer mechanisms for transatlantic policy coordination.

The "New Transatlantic Agenda" of Madrid

All these arguments for and against new transatlantic structures have already been at the heart of talks between Europe and America. The considerable pressure of political expectation ultimately resulted in the signing of two new transatlantic documents at the Euro-American summit on December 3, 1995 in Madrid. Europeans and Americans agreed on the "New Transatlantic Agenda" and the "Joint EU-US Plan of Action."

In these documents the European Union and the USA had, for the first time, laid down in detailed and coherent form the whole spectrum of tasks they had to tackle through cooperation. There was mention of cooperation in restoring peace to the former Yugoslavia and in helping to create economic stability in Russia, as well as in setting up a transatlantic economic area and intensifying cultural cooperation. In general, the partners committed themselves to coordinating their efforts regarding support for peacekeeping, stability, democracy and economic development all over the world. With regard to bilateral trade, they agreed to conduct a joint study aimed at finding ways to reduce trade barriers. Furthermore, the documents listed a series of specific individual economic topics (such as cooperation between customs authorities) where efforts would be made to conclude bilateral agreements in the near future.

So does this new agenda constitute the groundwork for a transatlantic renaissance that is wanted by both sides? Answering this question with a resounding "yes" would be to expect too much of these new documents. However satisfying it may be that after a five-year gap, and as a result of German initiative in particular, a new strategic document detailing transatlantic cooperation has been adopted, it became very clear during the preparations for Madrid that there was still strong opposition on both sides to more binding forms of cooperation. For example, the new document did not include the "Transatlantic Free Trade Agreement" proposed by Germany and other states as a future goal. This was because the creation of such a free trade area might entail some European partners, and the USA, giving up their much-loved policy of awarding subsidies.

In terms of content the "New Transatlantic Agenda" lays extremely demanding foundations with its wealth of joint tasks. What it does not yet do, however, is solve the question concerning the underlying future orientation of the Transatlantic Community. There is not yet any indication as to how the high aspirations for common global challenges are to be translated into a corresponding organizational structure for cooperation between Europe and America.

Creating new structures

If one gives credence to the critics of founding transatlantic structures anew, the main reason why new forms of binding cooperation between Europe and America have not yet found their way onto the agenda lies in the fact that the degree of transatlantic common ground purportedly shrunk following the end of the Cold War. Under this hypothesis new levels of commitment are interpreted as voluntarist, placing too heavy a burden on existing structures in particular and thus contributing to their disintegration.

Does this render the idea of founding the Transatlantic Community anew obsolete, making it nothing more than an outdated illusion of harmony? If one studies the arguments of the critics closely, one comes to quite a different conclusion. Almost without exception, all the objections to new structures of cooperation focus on individual aspects of new models and bemoan their lack of feasibility and/or their detrimental effect on Euro-American relations. In most cases this criticism does not get right to the heart, or to the roots, of the discussion, namely the objective interest in and need for a new common direction in political, economic and social issues on both sides of the Atlantic. Beyond the individual proposals under discussion at the moment what is this need based on?

The answer can be found in closer analysis of the actual or purported lines of conflict between Europeans and Americans mentioned above. It is true that, when attempting to solve international crises, differences – and sometimes quite spectacular ones – between the transatlantic partners have often come to light. However, it is also true that in almost every international crisis the Europeans and Americans are capable of working towards a common aim against a common adversary and are usually the only parties capable of guaranteeing and implementing constructive solutions.

In Bosnia, Europeans and Americans stand side by

side against ethnic intolerance and aggression. With regard to Russia and Eastern Europe, they share the common goal of creating a democratic order based on the principles of the free market economy. In the Middle East the peace process would have no chance of success if it were not for the commitment of the Americans and Europeans with regard to security and economic policy. And last but not least, the joint efforts of both partners made an essential contribution to the successful conclusion of the Uruguay Round of GATT talks. Differences of opinion – both temporary and lasting – regarding the necessary approach to individual issues have emerged between the Europeans and Americans in the course of all the above. But these differences were not based on deeply entrenched transatlantic antagonism, but rather on the exigent demand for a common western strategy to respond to the challenges of international crises, a demand which could not always be satisfied in its entirety.

This essentially common approach to solving global conflicts and challenges cannot only be explained by the existence of a security alliance, namely NATO, that has ensured almost 50 years of security cooperation between Europeans and Americans. The common ground shared by the two partners goes way beyond the domain of this Alliance. The basis for cooperation rests on the shared understanding, which has been achieved over the decades, of the fundamental values and mechanisms of western democracies – in particular the building up of democratic structures in politics, administration and society, the respect of human rights (including those of national minorities), pluralism and market economics. An awareness of this common understanding and the successes that the Transatlantic

Community has achieved in the post-war era both on the respective home fronts and internationally is the source of present-day concern that failure to tend this common ground may lead to its gradual erosion and hence to the end of the transatlantic success story. And this concern gives rise in turn to the search for new ideas to extend successful cooperation into the future. Given the historically unprecedented cohesion of the Euro-American partnership, it is almost inevitable that Europe and America will act together in the future, too, and will continue their quest for a broad outline to govern this cooperation. This is where, over and above the individual proposals, the nucleus of the present discussion about a revival in transatlantic relations lies.

Listing the common ground should not, however, tempt us into assuming that the future of the Transatlantic Community will unfold of its own free will. The cooperation of the past 50 years was binding in its organization and structured according to an overriding idea thanks to the common security interest that prevailed. This was the nucleus around which the political action of the partners revolved and which always had to be considered when it came to other areas of cooperation such as dealing with transatlantic differences.

These experiences raise serious doubts as to whether the level of cooperation reached thus far can be maintained if the structure provided by security policy arrangements from the Cold War era slowly begins to crumble, without a new guiding principle and/or structure to take its place. Such a principle is not going to emerge simply by stringing together single points of a common agenda – a recommendation that has been made by some well-meaning critics of new forms of organization. It is not enough to present a list of topics indicating those areas where the transatlantic partners find themselves at the same side of the negotiating table or where there is particular need for clarification. What is required is a binding mandate for common action that structures the individual items on the agenda and provides the partners with a reliable frame of reference for the purposes of arriving at consensus.

Even supporters of transatlantic reorganization often point out the current lack of any agenda that even comes close to the challenge constituted by the Soviet threat after the Second World War. This argument underestimates the possible positive – but also negative – dynamics of the current political situation and the significance of pro-active strategies. With hindsight, the founding of NATO and the integration of the western community seemed an instinctive reflex action, so to speak, to Soviet expansionist posturing. Back then, the whole situation was regarded quite differently. Western integration and a binding security partnership had to be pushed through by politicians such as Konrad Adenauer, Robert Schuman and George Marshall in the face of – sometimes stiff – national and international opposition. There was still no evidence whatsoever to prove that a western community of action and values was feasible. Only the success of such a vision makes it so self-evident to us today. Today, we are playing for very high stakes indeed, namely the preservation of this community which can only be guaranteed by a for-ward-looking strategy aimed at founding the com-munity anew.

Founding the Transatlantic Community anew

The task of finding a new direction can certainly be compared to that facing the transatlantic partners after the Second World War, one which demanded a radical paradigmatic shift on both sides of the Atlantic. The founders of the post-war order were aware that this change of direction and the new quality of Euro-American ties they were striving to achieve was not possible if relations within the western community were only governed by loose arrangements. Despite the centuries of special relations between Europe and America, the gargantuan tasks of the post-war era could not have been solved with a mere informal gentlemen's agreement. The degree of organization within the western community had to be improved and this improvement found expression in the form of NATO (complemented by its economic counterpart, the Marshall Plan).

Today's new challenges, too, call upon the Euro-American partnership to take a great step forward in terms of commitment. The agenda is headed by the renaissance of the Transatlantic Community uniting the USA and the European Union. This task involves defining a clear vision of a continued transatlantic success story, in the face of different external conditions, that is obvious to both domestic and external observers and that will give all partners involved a highly exigent, common goal to work towards. Furthermore, the new community has to create an organizational framework that enables the diverse and far-reaching common traits of the transatlantic partners to be developed into a coordinated and well defined strategy for political action.

This rejuvenated community should thus become

both catalyst and framework for the development of a contemporary agenda for all those issues no longer covered by traditional structures. This would not only entail skill in solving technical problems but also, and perhaps more importantly, the readiness for complete and unqualified consultation and communication on both sides of the Atlantic. This demands both an entirely new willingness to learn on the part of the Europeans and Americans and a new degree of flexibility, and in particular calls upon them to bid farewell to their much-loved – but extremely restrictive – antiquated way of dealing with one another when it comes to trade policy or discussions on the sharing of international burdens, for example.

With respect to institutionalizing the Transatlantic Community, practical experience can be gleaned from transnational integration in Europe and elsewhere. Recent challenges would seem to indicate there is urgent need for action in the following three areas: 1. creating proper binding structures for political consultation, 2. overcoming limitations in trade policy by setting up a Transatlantic Common Market, and 3. exchanging experiences and information pertaining to the pressing, supranational problems facing western industrialized societies, in other words building up a transatlantic learning community.

In these three fields, cooperation must be fixed by binding transatlantic agreements. Furthermore, a general frame for the different fields of cooperation ought to be fixed in the form of a strategic agreement between Europe and the United States in order to establish a Transatlantic Community. Whether this framework convention is established as a transatlantic contract, a charter or a binding common declaration is of subordinate importance. It is more important to formulate an objective which is credible for politicians and society on both sides of the Atlantic and to refer to the institutional and organizational steps in order to implement this objective in the most important fields, which will be put in more concrete terms in the following.

New structures for political cooperation

Unlike during the period of East-West confrontation there is no all-encompassing raison d'être nowadays which can be relied upon when reestablishing the Transatlantic Community, as was the case in the past when all partners could count on the common security policy. The building up of new binding structures must therefore revolve around issues where the partners have an obvious interest in joint action as a matter of paramount importance.

If one considers the emphasis of European or American political action, this requirement is evident particularly in the coordination of strategy in response to global challenges and/or international crises. Nowadays, Europe and the USA remain the only reliable makers or guarantors of stability in the world. The variety of burning issues in international politics calls for action by the transatlantic partners on an almost daily basis and, of all places, in regions and areas where the existing institutions of the North Atlantic alliance have no jurisdiction. There is, as yet, no permanent coordination mechanism between Europe and the USA to deal with these issues. Now that the traditional security partnership has been somewhat watered down, however, there is an increasing danger that the fallout from these conflicts may affect the Transatlantic Community, too. What is more, this development has to be seen against the backdrop of greater navel gazing by both the USA and the members of the European Union as a result of problems and challenges at home.

Therefore, it is vital to set up a binding structure for transatlantic political consultation and cooperation that would give the transatlantic partners a reliable mandate to coordinate all issues that are relevant to the transatlantic agenda. When it comes to structuring this consultation and cooperation, use could be made of the experience gained from an extremely useful instrument of the European Community, namely European Political Cooperation (EPC), which was introduced in 1970 as the first permanent forum for coordinating the common policy of the members of the EEC, as it was then known. Back then, the European member states were simply taking into account the fact that, as a result of the growing political importance of the European Community, the challenges posed by international politics were increasingly calling for a pan-European response. Over and above their responsibility for trade and economic policy, the founding Treaties of the EEC provided for no additional political mandate. Hence the decision by the member states of the EEC to establish EPC as a step towards a joint mechanism responsible for the policy of the Community as a whole.

A decisive factor in the functioning and results of EPC was the fact that it not only instituted regular political coordination on all relevant international issues at a European level, it also resulted in the Europeans at least setting themselves the task of having a common position with which to respond to all these issues. Even when this was not always successful or when a common position merely reflected the European lowest common denominator, so to speak, EPC had a central role in developing political responsibility for Europe as a whole.

It is now time for the Transatlantic Community to institute a similar mechanism, to set up some form of Euro-American Political Cooperation (EAPC). This EAPC would be an appropriate forum for dealing with all the issues that the international community directs at the transatlantic partners but where no organizational form has yet been found to accommodate them. Pressing topics falling under the domain of this forum for political cooperation could be the coordination of common transatlantic strategies for tackling the main international challenges of the day such as furthering the peace process in the former Yugoslavia, promoting political and economic stability in Central and Eastern Europe and the Soviet Union's successor states, bringing about a peaceful solution in the Middle East or developing strategies aimed at tackling global environmental destruction or the dangers of terrorism etc.

Euro-American Political Cooperation would have to extend to all the multilateral forums, such as the United Nations, disarmament conferences, the World Trade Organization etc. All these organizations would have to set up transatlantic consultation groups as has been the practice for coordination within Europe for some time now.

The "New Transatlantic Agenda" adopted in Madrid on December 3, 1995 contains a well-structured catalog of topics requiring joint political consultation. All these pressing topics to be dealt with by the transatlantic partners are listed as objects of Euro-American efforts at coordination. This impressive agenda is further evidence of the imperative necessity to introduce the binding structure that would allow this coordination. The institution of Euro-American Political Cooperation would fit this description perfectly and, as a major factor in reestablishing the Transatlantic Community, is thus high on the agenda in the search for a forward-looking Euro-American strategy.

Creating a transatlantic common market

Nowhere is the level of existing transatlantic interdependency more visible than in economic relations. This policy area constitutes one of the central vehicles of previous – and future – progress in transatlantic integration. In this respect, great care must be taken to shape the political framework for this tightly woven network of relations in such a way that it becomes the catalyst driving integration forward and not – as has often been the case in the past – the brakes holding it back.

Europe and the USA boast the closest economic ties in the world. Some 42 percent of the 228 billion dollars invested by the USA abroad end up in the European Union, while total European (EU) foreign investment in the USA amounts to the equivalent of 248 billion dollars. This corresponds to 56 percent of all European foreign investment outside the EU. In total, some twelve million American jobs are dependent on foreign investment by the EU and America. This translates into around ten percent of total employment in the USA.

Foreign investment is the most visible sign of the dynamic interdependency of national economies or economic areas and the globalization of industrial production and services. Ties with Asia and the Pacific or Latin America, much maligned by the Americans, trail far behind in this respect. A mere 32 percent or so of American foreign investment is to be found in the states of the Pacific Rim and only 19 percent in Latin America.

While bilateral trade between America and the countries of the Asian-Pacific Rim may have overtaken America's trade volume with the European Union, its trade balance with the EU is at least in a state of equilibrium – something which cannot be said for America's trade relations with Asia and the Pacific; the United States is currently running annual trade deficits with Japan and China of 60 and 20 billion dollars respectively. This accounts for some 70 percent of the total US trade deficit and has led to the now severe friction over trade between the USA and this region.

The high degree of transatlantic economic interdependency somehow seems to evade the collective consciousness of the European and American populations. What they never fail to notice, however, are the recurring clashes over trivial matters such as bananas, feta cheese or spaghetti although the respective trade volumes in these goods account for a mere fraction of their governments' economic interests.

Likewise, unheeded by the public at large, countless negotiating teams of European and American officials in various different forums endeavor to thrash out progress concerning individual aspects of transatlantic trade such as liberalizing public procurement, standardizing product norms, dismantling export subsidies, etc. The specialist level of this dialogue and the closely woven network surrounding it are further evidence that, in Europe and the USA, the notions of market economics with respect to the framework and structure of economic systems are closer than anywhere else in the world.

If one measures the results of this dialogue on regulatory policy against dynamic potential and against the extent of real economic trade between Europe and America, though, a serious policy deficit emerges. Transatlantic settlement mechanisms lag way behind the supranational vitality of trade between Europe and America and hamper its further development in a manner that is seriously out of tune with the times. From complicated differences in product standards and norms, via differing testing requirements and safety standards to cunningly refined methods of protectionism in minute sectors of the economy, the free movement of goods, capital and services across the Atlantic is still hindered by a veritable battery of trade barriers.

Previous experience has demonstrated that it is difficult to eliminate deeply entrenched opposition to modernization from segmented individual interests using the normal channels. Removing existing barriers to trade can only succeed if Europe and America manage to make their removal part of a strategic vision and manage to win over the population by means of pro-active arguments. Such a strategy can be successful only if Europe and America categorically declare their faith in a revival of their trade relations. The founding of a Transatlantic Common Market, anchored in an agreement between the European Union and the USA, would be an optimum means of achieving this aim. This agreement ought to provide for specific objectives aimed at dismantling existing tariffs that hamper trade and, furthermore, formulate the timetable for a standardized Euro-American economic area, i.e. dismantle any barriers to trade caused by regulatory policy.

Objectors to the idea of a Transatlantic Common Market often hold that it, too, is a voluntarist notion, misusing economic relations as a replacement for crumbling security ties and, as such, as putty to hold the western community together. Such demands would, the critics claim, place too heavy a burden on transatlantic trade and indeed endanger its very substance.

Yet arguments such as these misunderstand the new initiatives. Finding a simple replacement for the security partnership as a way of creating a sense of togetherness is simply not on the agenda. It is precisely because this raison d'être is lacking that all existing forums have to channel their energies into transatlantic cooperation even more intensively than ever before. Because of their sheer volume, transatlantic economic relations have an important role to play in this respect. In the past their development has been neglected, not least because of the indisputable dominance of issues of security policy. Furthermore, the opening up of the former Communist states, the gradual dismantling of COMECON restrictions and keener competition with East Asia – not to mention competition to conquer it as an export market – have raised important new questions which urgently require a common response from the western community. Otherwise it runs the risk of endangering the capability and performance of both Europe and America as industrial locations.

A second objection to a Transatlantic Common Market focuses on the dynamics of growth prospects. Both the USA and the European Union can expect far more growth in their trade relations with the APEC (Asia-Pacific Economic Cooperation) states and Latin America – or so the argument goes – than in the volume of their transatlantic trade. If, for example, China and Japan relax their trade barriers – a development the USA is hoping APEC will have achieved by the year 2020 – this will trigger a dynamic spurt of growth in economic relations with these regions. Even now, some 90 percent of all transatlantic trade is already exempt from duties and tariffs so any initiative aimed at free trade in this area is, it is claimed, no longer worth the effort.

This line of argument confuses western wishful thinking with reality. A fascination with the markets of East Asia must not be allowed to hide the fact that opening them up and, in particular, guaranteeing their compatibility with western trading standards is an extremely laborious business. The experiences American intermediaries have gathered there in recent years make this quite plain. Moreover, the political heterogeneity of the region constitutes a constant risk even for markets that have already been tapped successfully, as the example of China demonstrates. It is therefore highly unlikely that a free trade area with the APEC countries will be achieved within the next twenty years. And just as improbable within this space of time are trade figures with this region on a par with those recorded within the Transatlantic Community.

Besides, one-sided concentration on the Pacific Basin obscures the view of the very real opportunities for growth in transatlantic trade. For example, the European share of total American foreign investment in the past twenty years has risen from around 30 percent to 42 percent while the corresponding figure for the Pacific Basin has fallen from 40 percent to 32 percent.

The anticipated progress in European integration, especially the introduction of a single currency and the accession of countries from Central and Eastern Europe, is likely to make the investment climate in Europe much more attractive for American enterprises. For its part, Europe needs all the support from foreign capital it can get in order to finance the mammoth task of economic reconstruction in the East. Therefore, if one looks closely, a fresh attempt at opening up European and American markets would prove an extremely profitable affair that could make a considerable contribution to guaranteeing future economic prospects on both sides of the Atlantic.

Founding a transatlantic learning community

The internal challenges facing the members of the transatlantic partnership increasingly require consultation between Europe and America, too. In the case of problems such as international crime, drug trafficking, migration etc., it is clear that there is a need for joint action. But many other issues, too, such as reform of social security systems or education only appear to have a national character. Increasingly, strategies aimed at solving these problems can draw on models from another society within the Transatlantic Community. Recently there have been many cases where Europe and America have looked to arrangements on the other side of the Atlantic as a source of important ideas and solutions for their respective domestic political problems.

By way of example, President Clinton's health care reforms were clearly inspired by European models. Even though Clinton was initially unable to push through his proposals, the topic is still set to remain on America's domestic political agenda. By the same token, American automobile emission levels were crucial for European policy-makers in this field, who had somewhat less experience in dealing with smog than their American counterparts. When it came to sulphur pollution and the ensuing dying of the forest, the boot was once again on the other foot; the Americans were able to make use of the results of specialist research conducted in Europe in the late seventies. The merits of the American higher education system and the results of top level research are put forward by European experts as important arguments in the debate on higher education reform in Europe. Many American educators and politicians have, in turn, pushed for certain elements of the German vocational training system to be adopted in the USA.

There are countless other examples to illustrate how the partners on both sides of the Atlantic are prepared to learn from the experiences of their opposite numbers. The globalization of economy, the media and cultural bodies means that social challenges in Europe and America are becoming increasingly similar. Nevertheless, because of their differing – and to a certain extent complementary – historical development both sides have a different approach to solving problems. This now creates the ideal conditions for founding a transatlantic learning community which would give some structure to the contacts and cross referencing that have, up to now, been somewhat random.

The conditions for this new form of community are currently extremely favorable on both sides of the Atlantic. While redefining themselves both Europe and America have seen the crumbling of structures that were long deemed to be entrenched. Bill Clinton's health reforms are just one example. In Europe, work on abolishing the long-standing state monopolies in the telecommunications and media sectors has begun in earnest. Monetary Union will provide a modernization boost of an extent that has been inconceivable up to now. In the process of these reforms both Europe and America should use the opportunity to become model societies for one another when it comes to solving internal problems. The up-and-coming transatlantic generation is no longer going to be content with solving problems of domestic policy by using the purportedly unshakable yardsticks of national or regional tradition, but rather is going to be interested in harnessing joint intellectual effort by means of transnational creativity to solve similar or identical problems in the respective societies. The Transatlantic Community has to provide the structures necessary for this form of intellectual exchange.

Recent examples taken from German-American relations demonstrate that this learning community has already been anticipated. In 1993, for example, the German-American Academic Council, i.e. a German-American Academy of Sciences, was founded. The Council is composed of renowned German and American academics who initiate projects aimed at finding common solutions to problems occurring on both sides of the Atlantic. Teams of German and American academics and outside experts are set up to develop strategies that can be implemented in both societies. Examples of issues currently under consideration by the Council are migration problems in Europe and America, promoting cultural awareness in times when public funding is in short supply and the structure of higher education and research in Germany and the USA.

One further example are the invitations extended by

the German Chancellor to leading personalities from American society to visit Germany for a two-week stay. Since 1988, this program has enabled around 70 leading American entrepreneurs, university vice-chancellors, editors-in-chief of major newspapers, presidents of foundations etc. to visit Germany and exchange ideas in detailed talks with the Chancellor. And many, for the first time, have been able to collect information about strategies used in Germany to solve problems in their specific professional fields.

In addition, the academic transatlantic dialogue has profited enormously from the three German financed Centers for German and European Studies that were set up in the three top-class American universities of Harvard, Georgetown and Berkeley in 1990 and 1991. These centers have enabled highly qualified American students to study German and European affairs as well as provided an excellent forum for academic exchange between leading European and American scholars. Particularly important in this respect is the fact that this approach has succeeded in providing leading American university professors and academics with an opportunity to get to know Germany and Europe over and above the traditional university exchange programs.

The initiative behind this project is based on the notion that new forward-looking motivation is required to induce representatives from various social groups to get to know their transatlantic partners. The present – still tightly-knit – network of international transatlantic links largely harks back to the logic of East-West confrontation. During the Cold War, interest in Germany and/or Europe and in America was given massive government support because these ties were deemed essential for shoring up the security partnership. European and American governments gave committed support to youth and student exchange programs, town-twinning and reciprocal visits by officials at all levels, in the hope that such cooperation would result in increased public acceptance of the joint defense burden. For their part, the Americans also felt that there was a need to immunize the Western European people against the feared influence of Communism.

In future, similar arguments will no longer be valid as justification for governments subsidizing such a wealth of exchange programs. There is already a strong tendency in America to cut funding for cultural exchange as a result of severe budget constraints. In the medium term, this may lead to the Germans or Europeans also cutting back their funding of similar projects, thus reinforcing the decline in cultural exchange.

For the strategic future planning of a transatlantic learning community this means that the future of international relations will no longer be governed by the raison d'être of the security partnership, i.e. by a so-called superior motive. In the future, such exchanges will have to serve a specific aim, i.e. make a practical contribution to the future lives of citizens on both sides of the Atlantic. Scholars, students, representatives from public life, culture and industry will have to seek contact with their transatlantic partners, primarily because such contact constitutes progress in opening up prospects for mastering personal or social challenges. Given the great degree of transatlantic interdependency and the similarity of the tasks facing both societies, there is also, in this new situation, a great need for exchange both in Europe and in America. It is the job of politicians to tap this potential appropriately, to create optimum space for it to unfold as creatively as possible and, in so doing, increase the acceptance of transatlantic relations among the citizens on both sides of the Atlantic.

In this respect new structures must be built up on a broad social basis. The first prerequisite for this is democratic, i.e. primarily parliamentary, legitimacy. Hence a transatlantic parliamentary committee ought to be set up consisting of representatives from the European Union and the USA with a mandate to support and design forward-looking transatlantic cooperation. Moreover, economic and social interest groups on both sides of the Atlantic have to be involved, too. A transatlantic economic and social committee consisting of the main associations from industry, trade unions and other social groups could become a significant vehicle for lasting international ties.

All these new social ties will be judged according to how they contribute to adjusting the Transatlantic Community to the tasks of the future. The answer does not lie in holding on to a past that is seen through rose-colored glasses and the ties that once bound the transatlantic partners. Instead, a new plan is needed, geared towards action and mastering the new challenges.

Using the opportunities
of a new beginning

Any analysis of the transatlantic circumstances and options brings us to a central dilemma. On the one hand – as indicated above – no other two regions in the world enjoy such close ties, characterized by friendship and shared common values as well as by political and economic efficiency as do Europe and the United States. On the other hand, the historical development of this alliance over the last fifty years makes it clear that without a revitalization of these ties, that is both forward-looking and geared towards the changing situation in the world, the two partners are inevitably bound to grow apart.

The closeness of the Transatlantic Community in recent decades has only been possible because the security partnership founded in the post-war era provided the necessary framework. In the future, this framework is no longer going to be available. Thus far, only the initiated have been able to discern the first tiny cracks in the superstructure, demonstrated by the sharp decline in the number of visits to Europe by American parliamentarians and the cutbacks in funding for transatlantic cultural exchange.

The tendency for Europe and America to drift further

apart unchecked is still being prevented by the tenacity of the institutions of the post-war order. No one seriously calls into question the existence of NATO, for example, although the reason for its inception, namely the threat from the East, while not having disappeared completely, has been reduced considerably. The after effects of cohesion during the East-West confrontation will be available to the transatlantic partners as spiritual armor for some time yet. The imminent celebrations commemorating the fiftieth anniversary of the Marshall Plan, the Berlin airlift and the founding of NATO will certainly make a contribution to this.

Furthermore, the potential for differences of opinion between the western partners following the end of the Cold War has decreased considerably. Constant points of friction over the appropriate reaction to the Soviet threat have disappeared. Compared to the controversy over the natural gas embargo against the Soviet Union or the deployment of new types of missiles in the eighties, the present state of transatlantic relations exudes considerable harmony provided one does not look too closely.

The risk of increasing transatlantic indifference on a scale to match the disputes of old is, however, the other side of the coin. Because the potential sources of friction in cooperation on close security policy have ceased to exist, dealing with one's partners seems less and less necessary and, given the other promising issues of everyday politics, is often seen as a tiresome obligation. In the USA, this tendency is already very clear among the generation of Congressmen elected for the first time in 1994. The vast majority of them devote their time and energy to the challenges of domestic politics and have little time for representatives from their transatlantic partners. In Europe, too, interest in American partners has increasingly suffered at the hands of the pressing issue of European integration, especially the implementation of economic and monetary union.

Thus, on both sides of the Atlantic, the everyday routine of politics is creating ever greater distance between what were once the closest of partners. If this tendency is not nipped in the bud once and for all, this slight indifference will sooner or later grow into more sharply defined differences in the perception of international politics and the strategies that ensue. This will only become visible as a serious problem for the two parties involved and for the transatlantic population when this difference in perception turns into conflict in the light of a concrete international challenge, such as peace-keeping in a crisis region of the world. The expectation that this conflict of ideas will still be able to be solved using tried-and-tested methods of long-standing trans-atlantic cooperation may be deceptive. Successful Euro-American conflict management rests on the per-manent agreement between policy-makers and public on a common direction. If this is lacking, or if everyday politics begins to prefer solving domestic problems at the cost of the partner (for example, in trade policy), then, in a serious case, the value of transatlantic con-sensus will no longer be evident to politics nor to public opinion. A failure to display solidarity and the break in the transatlantic culture of close political and social in-teraction, as well as in the complementary definitions of two separate identities could be the ultimate conse-quences.

Sooner or later all parties involved will thus have to ask the inescapable question of how transatlantic rela-tions can be placed on a new footing so as to face up to the future. The longer it takes to come up with an answer to this question, the more difficult a new beginning will be. The adoption of the "New Transatlantic Agenda" in Madrid in December 1995 was the first step. But the process has to be driven forward to take in new binding structures for Euro-American cooperation, particularly of a political, economic and social nature.

At the moment the opportunity for refounding the Transatlantic Community is still ripe. The latest discussions on a Transatlantic Treaty, a Charter or a "New Agenda" have made the major policy-makers in politics, industry and society aware of the need for new initiative. The generation of committed supporters of the transatlantic partnership from the days of the East-West conflict are still with us and involved in policy-making and opinion-shaping. That is why we have to make decisive use of these conditions for a new beginning right now.

No one should make the mistake of thinking that such a new foundation will be easy to build. It will require a lot of effort on both sides and, more specifically, new and unconventional strategies. At the moment, because of the dominance of internal issues, it is more difficult to gauge how much foreign policy strain Europe and the USA can take. Founding the Transatlantic Community anew would require both partners to open up unreservedly towards the other transatlantic partner in areas such as trade and economic relations, transfer of experiences in social affairs, etc.

In the medium and long term, these new forms of cooperation will give both sides entirely new chances for development. In the short term, however, they could lead to painful adjustments, especially for the guardians of certain individual interests. Transatlantic renewal requires Europe and the USA to change their attitudes to a degree that can certainly be compared with the reestablishing of relations after the Second World War. Citizens on both sides of the Atlantic have to be won over if this new beginning is to succeed.

It is only by opening up the Transatlantic Community to the challenges of the future that we can ensure its continued existence and an ongoing success story. Any attempt at preserving the status quo coupled with a transfigured romantic view of the past would be the surest way to guarantee the inexorable erosion of this partnership. Everything depends on our seizing the historic opportunity to found the Transatlantic Community anew before the emerging tendency to ignore solidarity means it slips through our fingers for good.

Bibliography

Abshire, David M./Burt, Richard R./Wodsey, James, R. (eds.): The Atlantic Alliance Transformed, Washington, D.C. 1992.

Adams, Willi P./Czempiel, Ernst-Otto/Ostendorf, Berndt et al.: Die Vereinigten Staaten von Amerika, 2 vols., 2nd revised edition, Frankfurt a. M. 1992.

Ash, Timothy Garton: Im Namen Europas. Deutschland und der geteilte Kontinent, Munich 1993.

Asmus, Ronald D.: German Strategy and Opinion after the Wall. 1990–1993, Santa Monica, CA. 1994.

Bertram, Christoph: Europe in the Balance. Securing the Peace Won in the Cold War, Washington, D.C. 1995.

Beyond 1992: U.S. Strategy Toward the European Community. The Final Report of the CSIS Steering Committee on the Strategic Implications of EC 1992, Washington, D.C., The Center for Strategic and International Studies 1992.

Blackwill, Robert D.: Warum Europa und Amerika zusammenstehen müssen, in: Frankfurter Allgemeine Zeitung, February 20, 1995.

Blackwill, Robert D.: Der geschwächte Riese. Amerikas Führungsrolle im neuen Zeitalter, in: Internationale Politik, vol. 50, no. 5, 1995, pp. 3–9.

Blackwill, Robert D.: Paper on the National Interests of the USA, Wye Conference, December 1, 1995, unpublished.

Bradley, Bill: Time Present, Time Past. A Memoir, New York 1996.

Brandon, Henry (ed.): In Search of a New World Order. The Future of U.S.-European Relations, The Brookings Institution, Washington, D.C. 1992.

Brenner, Michael: The New Congress and U.S. Policy Toward Europe, in: Internationale Politik und Gesellschaft, no. 4, 1995, pp. 341–356.

Brenner, Michael: German and American Foreign and Security Policies. Strategy Convergence or Divergence, Sankt Augustin 1994.

Brenner, Michael (ed.): Multilateralism and Western Strategy, New York/London 1995.

Brenner, Michael: De bon usage de Clinton pour Europe, in: Politique étrangère, vol. 59, no. 4, 1994/95, pp. 1027–1040.

Brzezinski, Zbigniew: A Plan for Europe, in: Foreign Affairs, vol. 74, no. 1(1995), pp. 26–42.

Calleo, David P.: L'Europe vue par les Etats-Unis, in: Politique étrangère, vol. 59, no. 4, 1994/95, pp. 1017–1025.

Calleo, David P. (ed.): From the Atlantic to the Urals. National Perspectives on the New Europe, Arlington, Va. 1992.

Calleo, David P.: Die Zukunft der westlichen Allianz. Die Nato nach dem Zeitalter der amerikanischen Hegemonie, Stuttgart 1989.

Cameron, Fraser/Ginsberg, Roy/Janning, Josef: The European Union's Common Foreign and Security Policy: Central Issues … Key Players. Strategic Outreach Roundtable and Conference Report. With a Summary of Discussion by Stuart Mackintosh, Strategic Studies Institute, Washington, D.C. 1995.

Clinton, William J.: A National Security Strategy of Engagement and Enlargement 1995–1996, Washington, D.C./London 1995.

Christopher, Warren: Post-Election Foreign Policy, in: Foreign Policy, vol. 98, no. 2, 1995, pp. 6–27.

Czempiel, Ernst-Otto: Weltordnung statt Eindämmung – auf der Suche nach einem neuen Selbstverständnis amerikanischer Außenpolitik, in: Dembinski, M./Rudolf, P./Wilzewski, J. (eds.): Amerikanische Weltpolitik nach dem Ost-West-Konflikt, Baden-Baden 1994, pp. 1–21.

Czempiel, Ernst-Otto: Weltpolitik im Umbruch. Das internationale System nach dem Ende des Ost-West-Konflikts, Munich 1993.

Czempiel, Ernst-Otto/Dahmer, Kerstin/Dembinski, Matthias/Kunka, Gerle: Die Weltpolitik der USA unter Clinton. Eine Bilanz des ersten Jahres, Frankfurt a. M. 1994.

Daase, Christopher: Der erweiterte Sicherheitsbegriff und die Diversifizierung amerikanischer Sicherheitsinteressen, in: Politische Vierteljahresschrift, vol. 32, no. 3, 1991, pp. 425–451.

Dembinski, Matthias/Rudolf, Peter/Wilzewski, Jürgen (eds.): Amerikanische Weltpolitik nach dem Ost-West-Konflikt, Baden-Baden 1994.

Debiel, Tobias: Die europäisch-amerikanischen Beziehungen 1985–1992, Münster 1994.

Deudney, Daniel/Ikenberry, John G.: After the Long War, in: Foreign Policy, no. 94, 1994, pp. 21–35.

Dittgen, Herbert: American Foreign Policy after the Cold War: The New Challenges, in: Internationale Politik und Gesellschaft, vol. 2 (1994), pp. 131–144.

Duke, Simon: The New European Security Disorder, New York/London 1995.

Estrella, Rafael: After the NATO Summit. New Structures and Modalities for Military Cooperation, in: North Atlantic Assembly, Defence and Security Committee: 1994 Reports, Brussels 1994, pp. 1–29.

François-Poncet, Jean: Toward a Directorate of Continents, in: Harry Brandon (ed.): In Search of a New World Order. The Future of U.S.-European Relations, Washington, D.C., The Brookings Institution 1992, pp. 53–71.

Frellesen, Thomas/Ginsberg, Roy Howard: EU-US Foreign Policy Cooperation in the 1990s: Elements of Partnership, CEPS Paper, no. 58, Brussels 1994.

Friedrich, Wolfgang-Uwe (ed.): Die USA und die Deutsche Frage 1945–1990. Frankfurt/New York 1991.

Fröhlich, Stefan: Die USA und die neue Weltordnung, Bonn/Berlin 1992.

Fröhlich, Stefan: Der Sicherheitsbegriff wird mehrdimensional. Amerikanische Vorstellungen auf dem Weg zu einer gesamteuropäischen Ordnung, in: Zeitschrift für Politik, vol. 40, no. 3, 1993, pp. 285–303.

Frye, Alton/Weidenfeld, Werner (eds.): Europe and America: Between Drift and New Order, New York: Council on Foreign Relations, Gütersloh 1993.

Fukuyama, Francis: Das Ende der Geschichte. Wo stehen wir?, Munich 1992.

Gaster, Robin/Prestowitz Clyde jr.: Shrinking the Atlantic: Europe and the American Economy, Washington, D.C. 1994.

Gebhard, Paul R.: The United States and European Security, in: Adelphi Papers, no. 286, 1994.

Garten, Jeffrey E.: A Cold Peace. America, Japan, Germany and the Struggle for Supremacy, New York 1992.

Gutjahr, Lothar: Globale Konfliktdämmung. Europas Rolle in der Neuen Weltordnung aus der Sicht der USA, in: S + F: Vierteljahresschrift für Sicherheit und Frieden, vol. 10, no. 2, 1993, pp. 85–88.

Haass, Richard N.: Paradigm Lost, in: Foreign Affairs, vol. 74, no. 1, 1995, pp. 43–58.

Hacke, Christian: Deutschland und die neue Weltordnung. Zwischen innenpolitischer Überforderung und außenpolitischen Krisen, in: Aus Politik und Zeitgeschichte, B 46/1992, pp. 3–16.

Hacke, Christian: Die Beziehungen zwischen den USA und Europa in den neunziger Jahren. Innenpolitische Entwicklungen und außenpolitische Handlungsoptionen, Hamburg 1990.

Haftendorn, Helga/Tuschhoff, Christian (eds.): America and Europe in an Era of Change, Boulder, CO. 1993.

Haftendorn, Helga: Eine schwierige Partnerschaft. Bundesrepublik Deutschland und USA im Atlantischen Bündnis, Berlin 1988.

Hamilton, Daniel: Jenseits von Bonn. Amerika und die Berliner Republik, Frankfurt a. M./Berlin 1994.

Hamilton, Daniel: USA und Europa: Die neue strategische Partnerschaft, in: Aus Politik und Zeitgeschichte, B 9/1994, pp. 13–21.

Hanrieder, Wolfram F.: Deutschland, Europa, Amerika. Die Außenpolitik der Bundesrepublik Deutschland 1949–1994, 2nd fully revised and extended edition, Paderborn/Munich/Vienna/Zürich 1995.

Harris, Owen. Der Zusammenbruch des "Westens", in: Europäische Rundschau, vol. 21, no. 4, 1993, pp. 31–40.

Harris, Scott A./Steinberg, James B.: European Defense

and the Future of Transatlantic Cooperation, Santa Monica, CA. 1993.

Harrison, Glennon J. (ed.): Europe and the United States. Competition and Cooperation in the 1990s, Armonk N.Y./London 1994.

Hellmann, Gunther (ed.): Alliierte Präsenz und deutsche Einheit. Die politischen Folgen militärischer Macht, Baden-Baden 1994.

Hellmann, Gunther: Die Europäische Union und Nordamerika nach Maastricht und GATT. Braucht die Atlantische Gemeinschaft einen neuen Transatlantischen Vertrag?, Internal Studies/Konrad Adenauer Foundation, no. 70, St. Augustin 1994.

Hennes, Michael: NATO, Europäische Union und der Zerfall im Osten, in: Gewerkschaftliche Monatshefte, vol. 45, no. 3, 1994, pp. 168–178.

Hoffmann, Hilmar/Maaß, Kurt-Jürgen (eds.): Freund oder Fratze. Das Bild von Deutschland in der Welt und die Aufgaben der Kulturpolitik, Frankfurt/New York 1994.

Holbrooke, Richard C.: America, A European Power, in: Foreign Affairs, vol. 74, no. 2, 1995, pp. 38–51.

Joffe, Jose: "Bismarck" or "Britain"? Toward an American Grand Strategy after Bipolarity, in: International Security, vol. 19, no. 4, 1995, pp. 94–117.

Junker, Detlef: Von der Weltmacht zur Supermacht – Amerikanische Außenpolitik im 20. Jahrhundert, Mannheim/Leipzig/Vienna/Zürich 1995.

Kahler, Miles/Link, Werner: Europa und Amerika nach der Zeitenwende – die Wiederkehr der Geschichte, Gütersloh 1995.

Kahler, Miles: Regional Futures and Transatlantic Economic Relations, New York 1995.

Kaiser, Karl: Die deutsch-amerikanischen Sicherheitsbeziehungen in Europa nach dem Kalten Krieg, in: Europa Archiv, vol. 47, no. 1, 1992, pp. 7–17.

Kaiser, Karl and Maull, Hanns W. (eds.): Deutschlands neue Außenpolitik, vol. 1: Grundlagen, Oldenburg 1994, vol. 2: Herausforderungen, Oldenburg 1995.

Kaiser, Karl/Schwarz, Hans-Peter (eds.): Die neue Weltpolitik, Baden-Baden 1995.

Kennedy, Paul M.: Aufstieg und Fall der großen Mächte. Ökonomischer Wandel und militärische Konflikte von 1500 bis 2000, Frankfurt a. M. 1991.

Kennedy, Paul M.: In Vorbereitung auf das 21. Jahrhundert, Frankfurt a. M. 1993.

Kissinger, Henry A.: Die Atlantische Gemeinschaft neu begründen, in: Internationale Politik, 50, 1994, pp. 20–26.

Kissinger, Henry A.: Die sechs Säulen der Weltordnung, Berlin 1992.

Kissinger, Henry A.: Die Vernunft der Nationen. Über das Wesen der Außenpolitik, Berlin 1994.

Koch, Jutta: Zwischen Profilsuche und Kompromißzwang. Zur außenpolitischen Diskussion in den USA, in: Blätter für deutsche und internationale Politik, vol. 39, no. 1, 1994, pp. 94–102.

Krupnick, Charles: Not What They Wanted. American Policy and the European Security and Defence Identity, in: Moens, Alexander (ed.): Disconcerted Europe, Boulder, CO. 1994, pp. 115–134.

Kugler, Richard L.: US-West European Cooperation in Out-of-Area Military Operations. Problems and Prospects, Santa Monica CA. 1994.

Kunkel, Christoph M.: Amerikanische Außenpolitik in den 90er Jahren. Hegemonialer Abstieg oder neue Weltführungsrolle?, Mosbach 1994.

Lenz, Günter H./Milich, Klaus J. (eds.): American

Studies in Germany. European Contexts and Intercultural Relations, Frankfurt a. M./New York 1995.

Lindemann, Beate (ed.): Amerika in uns. Deutsch-amerikanische Erfahrungen und Visionen, Mainz 1995.

Lindsay, James M.: Congress and the Politics of US Foreign Policy, Baltimore 1994.

List, Juliane/Nolden, Hans-Willi: Zerrbild Deutschland. Wie uns Engländer, Franzosen und Amerikaner seit der Wiedervereinigung sehen, Cologne 1992.

Menon, Anand: From Independence To Cooperation: France, NATO and European Security, in: International Affairs, vol. 71, no. 1, 1995, pp. 19–34.

Moran, Theodore H.: American Economic Policy and National Security, New York 1993.

Nelson, Mark: Transatlantic Travails, in: Foreign Policy, no. 92, 1993, pp. 75–91.

Nelson, Mark M./Ikenberry, John G.: A New Agenda for US-EC Relations (Report of the Carnegie Endowment Study Group on US-EC Relations), Washington, D.C. 1993.

Nye, Joseph S.: Bound to Lead. The Changing Nature of American Power, New York 1990.

Pontland, Charles: The European Community and the Eastern Challenge, in: Haglund, David G. (ed.): NATO's Eastern Dilemmas, Boulder, CO. 1994, pp. 159–180.

Petersen, John: Europe and America in the Clinton Era, in: Journal of Common Market Studies 32, 1994, pp. 411–426.

Pfetsch, Frank R.: Die Außenpolitik der Bundesrepublik Deutschland 1949–1992. Von der Spaltung zur Vereinigung, 2nd edition, Munich 1993.

Reinicke, Wolfgang: Deepening the Atlantic. Toward a New Transatlantic Marketplace? Gütersloh 1996.

Rielly, John E. (ed.): American Public Opinion and U.S. Foreign Policy, Chicago 1995.

Rieß, Cornelia B./Bortfeldt, Heinrich: Die deutsch-amerikanischen Beziehungen der Nachkriegszeit (1945–1993), Melle 1994, (Deutschland-Report 21 of the Konrad Adenauer Foundation).

Rudolf, Peter: Die strategische Debatte in den USA – Konsequenzen für die amerikanische Rolle in Europa, in: Außenpolitik, vol. 44, no. 2, 1993, pp. 111–119.

Rummel, Reinhardt: Atlantizismus – Reformaufgabe und Führungsauftrag, in: Europa Archiv 12, 1993, pp. 369–376.

Scherrer, Christoph: "America first!": Verlassen die USA Europa freiwillig?, in: Berliner Debatte Initial, no. 6, 1992, pp. 79–83.

Schlesinger, Arthur Jr.: Back to the Womb? U.S. Isolationism Has Risen Yet Again From The Grave. The New Republican Congress Threatens Wilson's and F.D.R.'s Magnificent Dream of Collective Security, in: Foreign Affairs, vol. 74, no. 4, 1995, pp. 2–8.

Schmidt, Peter/Rummel, Reinhardt (eds.): Factors in Building a Common Euro-Atlantic Approach to Regional Crises. Unanswered Questions and Stark Observations about Europe's and America's Common Capability to Preserve the Peace Purchased at Great Cost to Both, Washington, D.C. 1994.

Schweigler, Gebhard: Driftet die atlantische Gemeinschaft auseinander?, in: Internationale Politik, vol. 50, no. 6, 1995, pp. 53–60.

Schweigler, Gebhard: Die USA zwischen Atlantik und Pazifik, Ebenhausen 1994.

Schweigler, Gebhard: Die Außenpolitik von Präsident Clinton. Erste Konturen, in: Europa Archiv, vol. 48, no. 19, 1993, pp. 553–562.

Serfaty, Simon: All in the Family: The United States and Europe, in: Current History, vol. 93, no. 586, 1994, pp. 353–357.

Sichermann, Harvey: Winning the Peace, in: Orbis, vol. 38, no. 4, 1994, pp. 523–544.

Smith, Michael/Woolcock, Stephan: Learning to Cooperate: The Clinton Administration and the European Union, in: International Affairs, vol. 70, no. 3, 1994, pp. 459–476.

Smith, Michael: US-EC Perceptions. "The Devil You Know": The United States and a Changing European Community, in: International Affairs, London, vol. 68, no. 1, 1992, pp. 103–120.

Smith, Steven K./Wertmann, Douglas A.: Redefining U.S.-West European Relations in the 1990s. West European Public Opinion in the Post-Cold War Era, in: Political Science, vol. 25, no. 2, 1992, pp. 188–195.

Smyser, W. R.: The Europe of Berlin. On a New Division of Labor Across the Atlantic, Gütersloh 1995.

Smyser, W. R.: Deutschland gegen Amerika? Eine Bestandsaufnahme für die Zukunft, Freiburg 1992.

Stern, Fritz (ed.): Perspektiven der deutsch-amerikanischen Beziehungen, Munich 1990.

Vorländer, Hans: Europa nach den Revolutionen von 1989 aus amerikanischer Perspektive, in: Berliner Debatte Initial, vol. 5, no. 2, 1994, pp. 31–37.

Wallace, William: European-Atlantic Security Institutions. Current State and Future Prospects, in: The International Spectator 3, 1994, pp. 37–51.

Wallace, William: Toward Transatlantic Partnership. A European Strategy, Transatlantic Policy Network, Brussels 1994.

Wallace, William: Regional Integration. The West European Experience, Washington, D.C. 1994.

Weidenfeld, Werner: Das deutsch-amerikanische Verhältnis steht vor einer neuen Epoche. Ein atlantischer Kulturbruch droht, in: Focus 39/1995.

Weidenfeld, Werner: Ernstfall Europa: Der Kontinent braucht konzeptionelle Klarheit, in: Internationale Politik, vol. 50, no. 1, 1995, pp. 11–19.

Weidenfeld, Werner: Die Transatlantische Herausforderung, Bonn 1995.

Weidenfeld, Werner: Jenseits des Selbstverständlichen: Europa und USA brauchen einen Neubeginn, in: Europa Archiv 13/14, 1994, pp. 365–372.

Weidenfeld, Werner: Plädoyer für einen Transatlantischen Neubeginn, in: Neue Zürcher Zeitung, September 16–17, 1995.

Weidenfeld, Werner: Tätigkeitsbericht des Koordinators für die deutsch-amerikanische zwischengesellschaftliche kultur- und informationspolitische Zusammenarbeit, Bonn:
1988 Brücken über den Atlantik
1989 Freundschaft als Zukunftsgut
1990/91 Partnerschaft im Wandel
1992/93 Vor neuen Herausforderungen
1994/95 Neue Wege transatlantischer Partnerschaft.

Weidenfeld, Werner: Wir brauchen die Transatlantische Gemeinschaft, in: Frankfurter Allgemeine Zeitung, May 9, 1995.

Weidenfeld, Werner and Janning, Josef (eds.): Europe in Global Change. Strategies and Options for Europe, Gütersloh 1993.

Weidenfeld, Werner/Wessels, Wolfgang (eds.): Jahrbuch der Europäischen Integration 1994/95, Bonn 1995.

Westphal, Siegrid/Arenth, Joachim: Uncle Sam und die

Deutschen – 50 Jahre deutsch-amerikanische Partnerschaft in Politik, Wirtschaft und Alltagsleben, Bonn 1995.

Weston, Charles M.: Amerikanische Außenpolitik unter Clinton, in: Außenpolitik, vol. 45, no. 3, 1994, pp. 226–235.

Weston, Charles M.: Die US-Außenpolitik zwischen Kontinuität und Neubestimmung, in: Aus Politik und Zeitgeschichte, vol. 17/1995, pp. 13–21.

Williams, Phil/Hammond, Paul/Brenner, Michael J.: Atlantis Lost, Paradise Regained? The US and Western Europe after the Cold War, in: International Affairs, vol. 69, no. 1, 1992, pp. 1–17.